CREATING COUNTRY STYLE

CREATING COUNTRY STYLE

KATHERINE SORRELL

STYLISH IDEAS AND STEP-BY-STEP PROJECTS

RYLAND
PETERS
& SMALL

LONDON NEW YORK

SENIOR DESIGNER Sally Powell

DESIGNER Sarah Fraser

EDITOR Miriam Hyslop

PICTURE RESEARCH Emily Westlake

PRODUCTION Sheila Smith

ART DIRECTOR Gabriella Le Grazie

PUBLISHING DIRECTOR Alison Starling

First published in the United Kingdom in 2005
by Ryland Peters & Small
20–21 Jockey's Fields
London WC1R 4BW
www.rylandpeters.com

ISBN 1 84172 941 8

A CIP record for this book is available from
the British Library

Printed and bound in China

introduction

Whether you are about to embark on a head-to-toe makeover of your home or simply want to freshen up a few rooms, this book aims to help with both inspirational and practical ideas for introducing country style. In every chapter there are quick tips and more detailed projects, some of them instant and inexpensive, others a little more ambitious; but if you are good with your hands and have a little time to spare, you will find them all satisfying to make and attractive to live with.

Country style is a relaxed and easy-going aesthetic that is more about emotion – how your environment makes you feel – than sticking rigidly to a particular set of rules. So use this book as a guide, taking the elements to which you are drawn and adapting them to your home and your way of life. The result will be a look that is as timelessly appealing as it is unique to you.

country

Why decorate in country style? Most people's answer would be because it suits not only their home but also their way of life, for whether you live in an idyllic rural setting, by the coast or the middle of a city, there is something tremendously appealing about an interior that is warm and welcoming, individual and eclectic – a look that is simple, but that has its own charming sophistication. It is the very opposite of the grand, stuffy, keep-up-with-the-Joneses type of decorating where order, symmetry and neatness are paramount and you can't put a book down without feeling that you've made a mess. Instead, country style allows you to mix old and new with hand-me-downs and junk-shop finds, and to combine colours, patterns, textures, fabrics and accessories with gusto and laid-back informality. This is a look that reflects traditional styles, the beauty of the natural world and, ultimately, your own, personal sense of surroundings that is both practical and pleasurable.

style

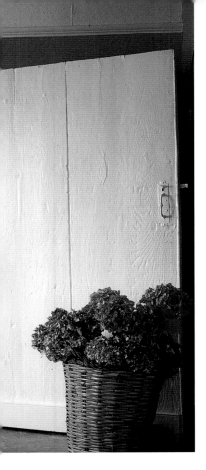

TOP ROW, LEFT TO RIGHT *A large-scale pattern of twining flowers in muted colours is typically English, and provides a lovely backdrop to an eclectic selection of furniture. Natural materials such as stone, wood and wicker are key elements of this style. For a highly feminine bedroom, choose floral walls teamed with a floral quilt and bunches of casually arranged fresh flowers.*

BOTTOM ROW, LEFT TO RIGHT *These tongue-and-groove cupboards are new, but fit perfectly with the traditional spindle-back armchair and the rise-and-fall lamp. Heavy curtains and a comfortable sofa upholstered in a wide check bring warmth and cosiness to this room. For the traditional look of a country bathroom, patterned ceramics and simple fittings, such as this shell-shaped soap dish, are ideal.*

English style

If you dream of a thatched cottage with roses around the door, chickens in the back yard and a cake baking in the range cooker, then English style is for you. Pretty as a picture and as unpretentious as it comes, it is comfortable without being lavish, charming without being fussy, and idiosyncratic without being eccentric (well, not too eccentric, anyway). It is a look that is never self-consciously fashionable, but never quite out of fashion, either. It is the look that evokes the England of cricket on the village green, strawberries and cream for tea, new-mown hay and church bells on a summer's evening. Harmonious and restful, English country interiors employ natural materials, honest furniture, pretty fabrics and a confident mix of colours, patterns and textures to create a rural retreat that instinctively appeals to all the senses.

American style

At the root of the American country style is a cheerful homeliness that reflects the early settlers' spirit of hard work, practicality and self-sufficiency. Sturdy, unembellished furnishings are mixed with bright and simple folk art and crafts – reminiscent of the familiar decorations of the settlers' varied European homelands. With function and comfort paramount, there are a few essential ingredients, some or all of which are usually found in every American country-style home: planked walls, a spindle-backed rocking chair, punched tinware, naïve paintings of people and farmyard animals, rag rugs and, of course, a boldly patterned patchwork quilt.

As a background, colours are predominantly cream and buttermilk, soft blue, verdigris, grey and earthy brown, plus an evocative 'barn red' made using oxides from the soil, in various shades from brown to russet. Colourful but down-to-earth fabrics complete the picture, creating a look that has survived centuries to inspire generations with its dignified, unfussy good looks.

TOP ROW, LEFT TO RIGHT *The functional appearance of this bathroom is softened by the bright, patterned rug and the Shaker-style chair in the corner. Cosy seating, colourful fabrics, a rag rug and naïve decorations – this comfortable sitting room has all the right ingredients. There's no mistaking the distinctive American patchwork quilt, here teamed with twin pencil-post beds, gingham curtains and a Shaker peg rail. Bold colours and traditional furnishings, including a pair of rockers, a spool daybed, a dough box and a pie safe, give this sitting room a timeless appeal.*

BOTTOM, LEFT *Simplicity is the key to this room, which is decorated with unfussy colours and natural materials.*

BOTTOM, FAR LEFT *The painted decoration is original to this renovated 1857 Texas ranch. Bold colours, such as this gorgeous deep turquoise, are quite common in American country homes.*

TOP ROW, LEFT *The mix of furniture styles here creates an eclectic look that is nevertheless coherent and easy on the eye, aided by the pale and pretty colour scheme.*

TOP ROW, CENTRE AND RIGHT *This simple white room, with its old beams and planked walls, could be almost anywhere and date from any time, but the toile de Jouy pillows add instant French style.*

BOTTOM, LEFT *Old-fashioned simplicity has enduring appeal, and this bathroom is no exception. Although as a whole it is quite spartan, there is generosity in the deep roll-top bath and a quirky luxury in the gilt-framed painting of a woman bathing.*

BOTTOM, RIGHT *This carved dresser is a lovely example of French design: elegant, pretty and practical all at the same time.*

French style

French style is, undeniably, the most chic and sophisticated of all the country styles, and yet it can easily be adapted to any home, from a humble farmhouse to an imposing chateau. Despite being a mix of antique and new furnishings, flea-market finds and objets d'art, this is a look that is effortlessly harmonious and cohesive, the imaginative mix of pieces being unified by their effortless prettiness. In the scroll of an arm, the curve of a chandelier, the carving of a frieze, the painted decoration of a jug, there is always an uncontrived elegance and lightness of touch. Classic Louis-style furniture is a good starting point for this look, combined with more rustic pieces such as dressers, armoires and side tables. Colours are pale and interesting, including cream, dove grey, taupe, stone, mid-blue and lemon yellow, with fabric including either exuberant Provençal prints or more sophisticated monochrome toile de Jouy.

Scandinavian style

Scandinavian country style is marked out by its combination of simple charm with understated grandeur, warmth and unpretentiousness with elegance and an uncluttered sense of space and light. In the typical Scandinavian country interior, an appreciation of traditional craft skills such as carving, painting and weaving combines with a use of natural materials and lively colours to create an interior that is both honest and original. Perhaps the best-known individual Scandinavian style, however, emerged in the late 18th century under King Gustav III of Sweden: known as Gustavian style, it is a blend of strict neo-classicism and Rococo gaiety with a gentle, accessible individuality, using subtle, pale colours, gilding, mirrors, delicate wooden furniture, glass chandeliers and floral swags. Neither prescriptively urban nor rural, it is a look that transcends place, class and time, as pretty and practical in a modest home as in a palace, and as distinctive and delightful as it was 250 years ago.

ABOVE, FAR LEFT AND LEFT *An uncluttered airiness makes this style distinctive, while pale colours and patterned textiles bring softness and comfort.*

ABOVE, CENTRE *White-painted floorboards are clean and fresh and reflect light beautifully.*

ABOVE, RIGHT *Checked fabric in a primary colour is typically Scandinavian.*

ABOVE, FAR RIGHT *This simple blue runner is Swedish and dates back to the 1930s, setting the scene for a timeless Scandinavian bedroom.*

BELOW *A sense of calm prevails here, thanks to a strictly limited colour palette, plain furnishings and minimal accessories.*

RIGHT *This cosy room features a pleasant combination of wood-planked walls, a frivolous chandelier and quality furniture with squashy upholstery.*

country

Colourful or neutral, pretty or plain, the timeless, enduring appeal of country style – whether American or European – extends throughout the house. From the entrance hall to the back door, the attic to the basement, you can add the relaxed charm of country style to every corner. In the living room, you can create an informal space that is welcoming, cosy and convivial, while the bedroom will be softly comfortable, calm and relaxing. The country-style bathroom is as functional as you need it to be, while also nurturing and indulgent; in the dining room, it is warm and inviting and in the kitchen, the heart of every country home, it comes into its own as a functional, appealing focal point for family life.

rooms

Warm and welcoming, relaxing and inviting, the country-style living room is a cosy, informal space in which to put one's feet up in front of a roaring fire. The key elements are soft colours, an harmonious mix of gentle patterns and a subtle blend of appealing textures. Furniture is unfussy and a squashy sofa is a must, covered with a scattering of pretty cushions

living rooms

and perhaps a cosy throw or two, co-ordinating with gathered curtains or plain blinds. On the floor might be wooden boards with ethnic rugs, a tactile carpet or nubbly natural matting. Planked or panelled doors complement walls covered in either tongue and groove, matt emulsion or delicate wallpaper, while finishing touches might include paintings and prints, mirrors, collections of china or wooden objects, photographs and, of course, vases of fresh flowers.

CLOCKWISE FROM CENTRE *Sew a deep hem along the long edge of a pretty tea towel and thread it over a slender pole for an informal (and inexpensive) window treatment. The gentle colours and simple pattern of this woven carpet make it a lovely choice. Make cosy chair cushions from square fabric remnants (it doesn't matter if they don't match exactly), sewing a pair of long ties to each corner to attach them easily. A mix of informal patterns really helps to create the look; adding cushions and throws to a comfortable sofa is a good way to start. A series of prints looks fantastic when framed identically and hung in a neat row. If you choose a monochrome colour palette, as in this all-white living room, introduce a variety of textures for interest and appeal.*

colours & textures

A country-style living room could be relatively plain, using cool, calm and neutral colours that don't draw attention to themselves, or it could be rich and intense, filled with bold shades that bring warmth and vibrancy. Texture, too, is highly important, as with texture comes sensuous appeal and an easy sense of comfort.

Start by considering your walls and floor, the largest surfaces in the room and therefore the areas that will have the biggest and most immediate impact. For this look, uneven and imperfect finishes are fine, perhaps even desirable. Walls could be bare brick or plaster, wood panelling or tongue and groove, or you may prefer patterned wallpaper. With painted walls, you could add decorative borders of paper or stencilling, or try your hand at a broken paint-effect such as stippling, spongeing or ragging. On the floor, fitted carpets are warm and cosy, while natural floorcoverings such as jute, sisal or coir have a suitably rustic appeal. Brick, stone, tiles or wooden boards are all attractive and an effective base for

OPPOSITE, TOP LEFT *In a neutral scheme such as this, textural contrasts provide a great deal of the interest, and despite its plain colours and relative austerity this living room is very appealing. There's a nice balance of hard and soft surfaces, with the carved detailing of the cupboard doors adding a pretty finishing touch.*

OPPOSITE, TOP RIGHT *Natural colour schemes can be very calm and serene. This light-filled room has a quiet charm and looks very comfortable.*

OPPOSITE, BELOW *Pale colours predominate in this pretty room, which has a lovely range of natural materials that make for appealing textural contrasts. The terracotta-tiled floor has a gorgeous warmth that is emphasized by its juxtaposition with off-white-emulsioned surfaces and cushions in subtle shades.*

The dark paintings make an intriguing contrast.

RIGHT *This boldly patterned wallpaper makes an eye-catching backdrop in this rather grand country living room. Plain colours are used elsewhere, picking up the colours of the paper, along with natural wood and metal.*

BELOW *If you choose neutral walls and floors, you can inject dashes of colour and texture in the form of painted-wood furniture – the more distressed, the better. A dresser might not seem an obvious item to place in the corner of a living room, but here it provides a perfect way of displaying a collection of simple, rustic crockery. The chest makes a great informal coffee table.*

LEFT *This simple scene shows just how effective a pleasing mix of textures can be.*

ABOVE *You can't beat the warmth of a wall painted in earthy reddish-brown, a natural colour that is ideally suited to a country interior. Here, it is highlighted effectively by simple, pure white upholstery.*

RIGHT *The indigo/turquoise paint on these walls has been sponged on for a dramatically mottled effect and has a look that is both informal and inviting. Vivid colours have been added in the form of the bolsters and throw on the sofa and the bold paintings. The overall look is intense and personal, but not overwhelming.*

this look, but you will undoubtedly want to soften them with an assortment of rugs.

These key areas provide you with the textural and colour backbone of your scheme. So, for example, pale and neutral schemes might involve the grey patina of stone, limewashed wood, cream-painted walls and unbleached cotton, while brighter schemes may use chintzy wallpaper and fabric, deep paint colours and polished, dark wood.

Use furniture, soft furnishings and accessories to enhance your basic scheme. For an elegant look, choose plain colours that harmonize and complement so that the whole room is based around a variation of just one or two shades; for a more eclectic, dynamic look, a varied range of colours and patterns can be exciting. Textural contrasts arise quite naturally – by putting a wicker basket on a wooden floor next to a velvet-covered armchair, for example – but there's no harm in taking some time to think about textures with a little extra care to ensure that the overall feel of the room is truly inspiring and inviting.

PROJECT 1

display frame

Frames are not especially difficult to make, though you will need the right tools and a little time and patience, as accurate measuring, sawing and mitring are vital. This simple box frame is ideal for displaying a collection of small treasures, perhaps pressed leaves or flowers, shells or feathers, for example. If the soft gilt finish doesn't suit your room scheme, simply give the box a coat of ordinary emulsion paint in a suitable colour.

MATERIALS & EQUIPMENT

12.5 x 25 mm (½ x 1 in) softwood, 800 mm (32 in) length, for front

38 x 125 mm (1½ x 5 in) softwood, 800 mm (32 in) length, for sides

hardboard, approximately 125 x 125 mm (5 x 5 in), for backing (cut to fit)

picture glass, cut to fit

tenon saw • mitre box • wood glue

4 mitre cramps or framing cramps

4 corrugated fasteners

hammer • panel pin • G-cramps

4 metal framing clips

2 ring and eye fittings

picture wire

red ochre emulsion • gilt cream

broad artist's brush

medium sandpaper • 2 soft cloths

1 Use a mitre box and tenon saw to cut the narrower softwood into four equal 150 mm (6 in) lengths, mitring the corners at 45°. Glue the pieces together at the corners to form the flat front of the frame. Clamp until the glue has dried and reinforce the joints with corrugated fasteners before removing the cramps (see page 104).

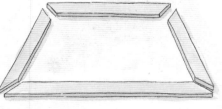

2 Using the mitre box and tenon saw, cut the 38 x 125 mm (1½ x 5 in) softwood into four equal lengths of 150 mm (6 in), mitring the corners at 45°. These lengths fit together to form a deep box that is attached to the back of the flat frame.

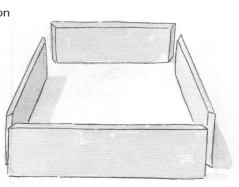

3 Glue the four sides of the box together and clamp the corners until the glue has bonded.

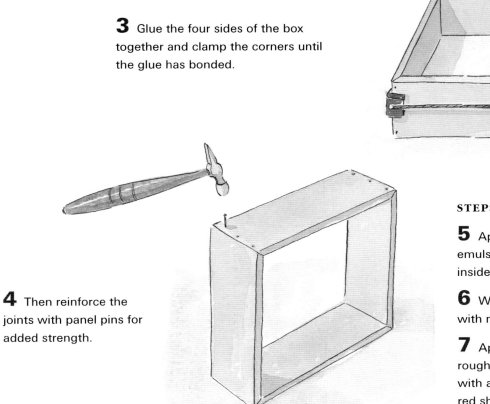

4 Then reinforce the joints with panel pins for added strength.

STEPS TO PAINT

5 Apply a base coat of red ochre emulsion to the front, sides and inside edges of the box.

6 When dry, roughen the surface with medium sandpaper.

7 Apply the gilt cream to the roughened surface, rubbing it in well with a soft cloth so that some of the red shows through.

8 When dry, polish to give a shiny finish.

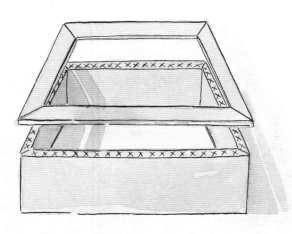

9 Glue the flat frame front onto the deep box and clamp until bonded.

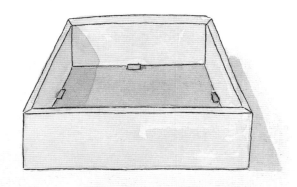

10 Cut the hardboard to fit and have a glazier cut the picture glass. Secure with metal framing clips and attach picture wire to hang the frame.

fabrics

OPPOSITE, TOP LEFT AND RIGHT *When combining patterns, choose colours that either match or are from the same family (pale blues with dark blues, for example). Florals are easier to mix with stripes and checks than with other florals.*

OPPOSITE, CENTRE LEFT *A sofa upholstered in a bold floral fabric is always eye-catching. Here, it is teamed with a white-painted floor and another sofa in plain chocolate, so the effect is pretty but laid-back and modern.*

OPPOSITE, CENTRE RIGHT *The plain upholstery of this sofa is an easy backdrop on which to throw an assortment of cushions. Hung from a metal pole, the gathered curtain is quietly complementary.*

BOTTOM ROW, FROM LEFT TO RIGHT *To jazz up a plain wooden chair, it's easy to make a floral chair pad, adding long ties for a pretty, country effect. These checked cushions are large and soft, and look highly inviting to sink into. To make a set of informal cushion covers, simply sew plain squares of felt together, using blanket stitch around the edges. More or less any sofa can be disguised with a large throw and piles of cushions.*

Fabrics play a key part in setting the scene for a country-style living room, bringing warmth, softness and a cosy sense of comfort, as well as a variety of appealing colours, patterns and textures. In general, it's best not to try too hard to co-ordinate fabrics, as a lived-in, unstudied mix will give a nicely informal effect – and if they appear gently worn, so much the better.

Your top priority, generally, will be to choose curtains, sofa covers and cushions, though you may also have chair covers, bolsters, tablecloths, throws, blinds, lampshades and wall hangings to consider, too. Try to maintain a balance between fashionably unfussy, streamlined soft furnishings and the frilly prettiness that is typical of country style. Curtains, for example, could be generously gathered, perhaps with trimmed edgings or contrasting borders; upholstery should be straightforwardly shaped, with valances and buttoning but no unnecessary flounces; and loose covers or large throws can do wonders to transform tired or unsuitable furniture.

Cotton (plain and twilled), canvas, muslin, linen and wool are all good basic fabrics; for extra interest you might consider felt, denim

FAR RIGHT *A combination of sunny yellow and deep crimson makes this a very inviting corner. The velvet cushions are really cosy and tactile.*

RIGHT *This checked blind has a pleasantly informal feel that complements the soft cushions on the seat below.*

BELOW *Patchwork has an eternal, informal appeal. Here it has been used as a cover for a sofa that's piled high with cushions in various fabrics, colours and patterns.*

velvet, silk or mohair – how heavy, hard-wearing and dirt-resistant the fabric needs to be will obviously depend on what you're using it for. Plain colours are a good starting point, but for many people this look is dramatically enhanced by introducing patterns. You might consider tweed, for example, with its interesting weave and subtly intermixed colours, or tartan for a bright, warming effect. Gingham, narrow stripes or tiny spots are subtle yet interesting, while chintz, paisley, tapestry, windowpane checks, broad stripes and floral or geometric patterns will make more of a statement. You don't have to stick rigidly to a fabric's intended or original use – a lightweight rug might be ideal to throw over the back of a sofa, for example, or a woollen blanket to gather up as a warm, thick curtain, while fabric remnants can be gathered together and made into a length of patchwork, the ultimate country fabric, which could be used for anything from an armchair cover to a window-seat cushion.

PROJECT 2

linen cushion cover

Freshen up a tired sofa or armchair with a new cushion or two in a style that is elegant yet unpretentious. This cover is very easy to make – two squares of linen with pairs of ties on each side sandwich an inner cover made from a contrasting fabric. It looks charming in these beige and red stripes, but any relatively lightweight fabric could be used, as long as you ensure that the inner cover complements the outer one effectively.

MATERIALS & EQUIPMENT

60 cm (24 in) beige striped linen fabric, 115 cm (45 in) wide

50 cm (20 in) red striped cotton fabric, 115 cm (45 in) wide

500 cm (192 in) cotton tape in brown, 2.5 cm (1 in) wide

500 cm (192 in) cotton tape in cream, 1 cm (½ in) wide

45 cm (18 in) square cushion pad

1 For the outer cushion, cut out two pieces of fabric from the striped linen, each 55 cm (22 in) square. Make sure the stripes run parallel with two of the sides.

2 Take one of the pieces and fold in 5 mm (¼ in) all round, overlapping the corners. Then fold in 2 cm (¾ in) and press, making sure the stripes match up on the wrong side of the fabric. Repeat for the other piece.

3 To make the ties, place the narrow cream tape in the middle of the brown tape and machine-stitch as close to the edges of the narrow tape as possible to secure together. Cut into 16 strips of 30 cm (12 in) lengths and press.

4 Lay one of the squares wrong side up and tuck one length of tape right side up 13 cm (5 in) from each corner, under the pressed edge. Pin ties in place.

5 To secure the ties to the cushion cover, machine stitch as close as possible to the inner edge of the turned-in seam, sewing across each of the ties. Make sure that the ties are straight.

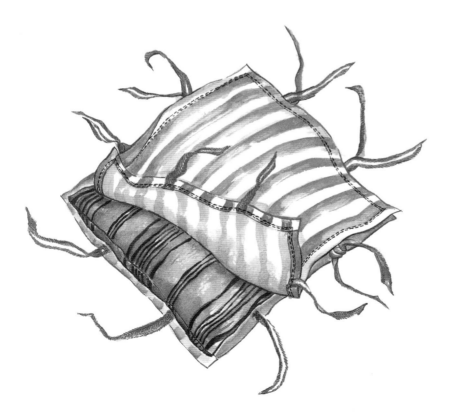

6 Fold each tie over the seam and press. Machine a second line of stitching 5 mm (¼ in) in from the inner edge to secure the ties facing outwards. Press. Repeat to attach the ties to the other square. Slip stitch (see page 105) each open corner closed and trim the ends of ties on the diagonal.

7 To make the inner cushion, cut out two pieces from the red striped cotton, each 48 cm (19 in) square. Lay the squares right sides together. Pin, baste and machine-stitch a seam line 1 cm (½ in) in from the outside edge around three sides.

8 Turn the cover right side out and press. Insert the cushion pad and slip-stitch the opening to a neat close.

9 Place the inner cushion in the middle of one outer panel (wrong side up), then put the other panel over it (wrong side down) and tie up to close.

LEFT *The focal point of this sitting room is undoubtedly the fireplace, with its imposing portrait above and pair of urns arranged symmetrically on the mantelpiece. The huge wicker basket alongside is used for storing logs, but is also a decorative piece in itself.*

BELOW, LEFT *Use herbs and foliage rather than formal cut flowers to scent and colour a room. And think laterally about containers – a metal pitcher, glass milk bottle or painted ceramic pot are all just as pretty as a 'proper' vase.*

BELOW, CENTRE *Bowls of snipped herbs and flower petals add a colourful, fragrant touch.*

BELOW, RIGHT *Chopped logs can be a feature in their own right, and this beautifully patterned bark is certainly worth including as a textural contrast – it's almost a shame to burn them.*

OPPOSITE *The old glass in this overmantel mirror simply adds to its attraction, and it fits well into this homely living room, where old fire irons are propped against the fireplace and stencilled decorations have been used to enhance the walls above the built-in cupboards.*

finishing touches

Country style can be plain and simple but it is never stark or severe, and even just a few carefully chosen finishing touches can transform an uninviting room into one that is warm and comfortable, informal and welcoming.

The fireplace is often the focal point of a living room, and a log basket or coal scuttle will probably be a necessity rather than an accessory. Add a set of old-fashioned tools propped casually alongside, and you have a look that is timeless and enduring, found in rural properties from the tiniest of cottages to the grandest manor house. And above the fire surround it is traditional to hang or prop either a large, gilded mirror or a painting. If you have room on top of the surround you might want to arrange a few accessories, such as candlesticks, vases or family photographs. In fact, photographs can

BELOW, LEFT *The plain shades of small table lamps can easily be embellished with ribbons, braid, buttons or feathers. Alternatively, you could stencil or paint on a motif.*

BELOW, RIGHT *Books really do furnish a room, and there's nothing to beat the whimsical charm of a set of old Penguin paperbacks.*

OPPOSITE, ABOVE *A small collection of glassware, some robust, some more refined, is displayed to advantage on a table by a window, where the light emphasizes the delicacy of the material. The display of foliage is also highly striking.*

OPPOSITE, BELOW, FROM LEFT TO RIGHT *Casual arrangements of flowers – perhaps hand-picked from your garden –*

look very sweet displayed in unusual containers, such as an old preserving jar. This wooden candle box is a useful storage piece but also looks delightful and is the sort of accessory that adds authenticity to any country-style scheme. Decorations need not be expensive – these hand-pressed leaves make an appealing feature, yet cost nothing.

be gathered on any available surface, along with glassware and ceramics (floral-printed, spongeware or blue-and-white crockery are all charming) or wicker baskets of all shapes and sizes – useful for storage as well as attractive in themselves.

Rows of old hardback books, or Penguin classics with their distinctive, graphic covers, add a lived-in feel, while on the walls you could hang framed needlepoint samplers, equestrian prints or woodblock illustrations, as well as drawings and paintings.

Display collections on shelves or windowledges and, if you are lucky enough to own one, you might

want to place a family heirloom, such as a wooden rocking horse, a hand-made doll's house or a grandfather clock in a convenient spot. Position a selection of charming lamps on side tables or shelves around the room – you could, perhaps enhance their shades with personal touches such as a stencilled motif or a trim made from ribbon, feathers or buttons. Finally, for a real scent of the countryside, use boxes and bowls to hold pine cones and pot pourri, and arrange cut flowers, foliage and herbs informally in simple containers such as jam jars or enamel pitchers.

PROJECT 3

pumpkin display

Hollowed-out pumpkins lit by candles placed inside make a wonderful Halloween display, their crudely carved faces once believed to ward off evil spirits. As an alternative autumn display, perhaps to be used as a table centrepiece, pumpkins make perfect natural containers for foliage, berries and candles. This project is very quick to complete and needs hardly any equipment or materials – you could quite easily use a selection of fruit and leaves from your own garden.

MATERIALS & EQUIPMENT

pumpkin, approximately 18 x 22 cm (7 x 8½ in) diameter

1 block floral foam, 8 x 11 x 8 cm (3 x 4½ x 3 in)

3 sprigs rosehips (*Rosa*)

5 sprigs blackberries (*Rubus fruticosus*)

5 sprigs guelder rose (*Viburnum opulus*)

8 sprigs fruiting ivy (*Hedera*)

3 purple beeswax candles, 25 x 2.5 cm (10 x 1 in) diameter

knife • spoon • medium-gauge florist's wire • wire cutters

tape • florist's scissors

1 Using a sharp knife, cut out a neat square in the top of the pumpkin, measuring 8.5 x 8.5 cm (3¼ x 3¼ in). Lift off the top and then use a spoon to scoop out the flesh inside to a depth of about 12 cm (4¾ in).

2 Thoroughly soak the block of floral foam in water, then insert it snugly into the pumpkin, pushing it down so that the top edge is flush with the surface of the pumpkin.

3 Cut six pieces of medium-gauge florist's wire, approximately 10 cm (4 in) long, and bend each one in half to form a hairpin shape. Tape two U-ends onto the base of each of the three candles.

4 Place the three candles in a triangular formation in the block of floral foam, anchoring them in place with the wires.

5 Cut all the foliage into sprigs of approximately 15–20 cm (6–8 in). Arrange the rosehips around the candles, pushing the stems into the floral foam.

6 Add the sprigs of blackberries and guelder rose in the same way, spacing them evenly over the arrangement.

7 Finally, use the sprigs of fruiting ivy to fill in all the gaps between the other berries, making sure that all the floral foam is concealed and that the display is a good shape with an even balance of colour.

PROJECT 4

autumn wreath

Rich red and orange beech leaves have been used to construct this beautifully glowing autumn wreath that would look fantastic either hung on a front door or else simply propped up on a shelf or mantelpiece. Use glycerined leaves, available from specialist florists, as this method of drying plant materials captures seasonal colours and prevents dried leaves from becoming dull and brittle, so that they will look stunning for six months or more.

MATERIALS & EQUIPMENT

for a wreath 50 cm (20 in) in diameter:

30 lengths honeysuckle vine (*Lonicera*),
1.6 m (5 ft)

20 branches glycerined beech leaves (*Fagus*)

florist's scissors • reel wire • wire cutters

medium-gauge stub wires

heavy-gauge stub wire

1 To make a circular frame, bend 30 lengths of flexible honeysuckle vine into a circle. As you work, bind the stems together with a continuous length of reel wire. Pull the wire taut to make the binding tight and secure.

2 Cut sprigs of beech leaves from the large branches, so their woody stems are about 2.5 cm (1 in) long. Arrange the sprigs in groups of three and wire them on double-leg mounts. To do this, hold a medium-gauge stub wire behind the group of stems and bend it into a hairpin, making one leg longer than the other. Wrap the long leg of wire around the stems and other leg of wire at least three times, then bring the wires together. Wire up about 150 sprigs into 50 bunches.

3 Hold a wired-up bunch of leaves, glossy side down, at an angle to the frame. Push the stub wires through the vine frame. Bend the group of leaves back on itself so that they face glossy side up. Tuck the wire ends into the back of the frame. Repeat with the next group of leaves, placing them 3 cm (1 ¼ in) from the first group so that they overlap.

4 Continue working in the same direction, adding groups of wired-up leaves every 3 cm (1 ¼ in) and turning the wreath as you go. In addition to attaching bunches along the top edge, start adding groups of beech leaves to the left and right of centre, to fill in the inner and outer edges of the frame.

5 As you work, introduce a mix of different-coloured beech leaves here and there to make the display look as natural as possible.

6 When you have worked your way around the frame, check for gaps and fill them in where necessary. Gently lift the leaves away from the frame to make the display look fuller. To hang the finished wreath, insert a heavy-gauge stub wire through the wreath back and twist the ends together. Dust at regular intervals to keep the display looking its best.

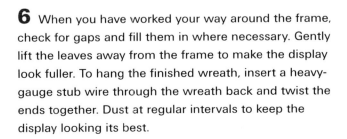

Cosy enough for an intimate supper for two, but spacious enough for a family meal or Sunday lunch with friends, a country-style dining space can suit more or less any occasion. The first requirement is a large, unpretentious wooden table. Next, a selection of chairs, ladder- or spindle-backed, rush-seated or upholstered – and they don't necessarily have to match. Gentle but adequate lighting will set the scene: either a chandelier or an old-fashioned rise-and-fall lamp would be a good choice, or you could

dining rooms

opt for the flickering glow of candles. Underfoot, durable, wipe-able flooring is most practical, but it needn't be boring – oiled or painted floorboards are lovely. And on the walls, pale colours will make the room seem airy and light, while darker shades add atmosphere and drama.

TOP, LEFT *This circular table is simple and charming, while the central pendant adds a gentle glow at night.*

TOP, RIGHT *Rush-seated chairs and a handful of ceramic accessories bring a farmhouse atmosphere even to a room that is otherwise rather bare.*

BOTTOM, LEFT *Differing patterns of checks and stripes in a toning colour add a charming variety to this dining room. It would be easy to make loose*

seat covers such as this, adding extra-long ties as a quirky decorative feature.

BOTTOM, CENTRE *Cover a dining table with a large piece of fabric (a sheet will do) for instant prettiness.*

BOTTOM, RIGHT *Mismatching chairs aren't a problem with this style, though if you prefer a more cohesive look you could always paint them all the same colour.*

colours & textures

Comfort is a priority in a dining room, as this is a space where you'll want to linger over a delicious meal in an atmosphere that's conducive to relaxation and enjoyment. Of course, everyone's idea of comfort is different, so for some a dining room should be decorated in fresh, pale colours to create a cool and airy feel; for others, deeper, bolder shades strike the right note of warmth and intimacy. Either style can look gorgeous and will fit perfectly with a country look.

When planning your colour scheme, remember that your dining table will be the focal point of the room. If you want to leave it uncovered, take your cue from the colour of its surface – pale or dark wood, sanded, polished or perhaps even painted, or covered with sticky-backed plastic. Paler woods such as beech and ash, or woods that have been limewashed or painted in a pale colour, tend to lend themselves to light and airy colour schemes, such as clean white, soft cream, dove grey, or a pale blue, pink, yellow or lilac.

TOP, LEFT *The blue and white chequerboard floor is the most eye-catching element of this simple dining room. It is fairly easy to create the same effect, using either linoleum or vinyl tiles, or by carefully painting wooden boards with two colours of floor paint.*

TOP, CENTRE *Deep colours can bring a great sense of comfort and intimacy to a dining room, and a bottle green such as this is highly effective, especially combined with the warm wood of the floor and furniture. The pale woodwork and checked fabrics offset the dramatic colour so that it is not overly imposing.*

TOP, RIGHT *There is something very appealing about an all-white dining room, probably to do with its associations of lightness and cleanliness. White can look very stark and modern, but here the furniture is traditional, the seats are padded and the twinkling chandelier above is delightfully traditional and pretty.*

RIGHT *There is a wonderful mix of textures in this room, from the stone floor to the linen blind, the wooden chairs to the white tablecloth. It is unforced and easy, a charming example of the country look at its best.*

LEFT *The deep reddish-brown on this wall has very earthy overtones and creates a strong impression – warm, dramatic and rather appealing. This may be an informal spot in which to have the odd bite, but it is nevertheless very inviting.*

ABOVE AND RIGHT *Vivid red and yellow have been used in this room as an accent against an otherwise neutral scheme comprising natural wood and white-painted walls. They add a note of vibrant good cheer to what is quite a formal setting.*

Darker woods, on the other hand, work extremely well with dramatic colours such as ochre, bottle green, navy or a classic 'dining room' red. Choose dining chairs that work with your theme – or, if you have chairs that don't quite look right, make loose covers for them using inexpensive fabric. Use paint or wallpaper to enhance the walls and, if your floor needs attending to as well, you can transform it quickly and easily either by painting boards with floor paint or throwing down a colourful rug.

Another way in which you can establish a welcoming atmosphere is by using contrasting textures, ensuring that you include enough softness – cushions, tablecloths, rugs, lampshades and window treatments – to counteract the hardness of tables, chairs and storage. Other textures will mix in easily – the glitter of cut glass, the glaze of ceramics, the shine of cutlery and the delicacy of fresh flowers – and the result will be a room that both looks gorgeous and feels delightful.

FAR LEFT, TOP *Making a patchwork tablecloth is a wonderful way to use up remnants of fabric, and it adds a cheerful, colourful note to any dining area.*

FAR LEFT, CENTRE *Checked fabrics in the same colourway always co-ordinate nicely, and look just right in a country-style dining room. This sweet little fruit container has been made by simply covering some cardboard with left-over fabric and adding ties at the corners.*

FAR LEFT, BOTTOM *Plump cushions add greatly to the comfort of this bench seat, and the understated fabric is a lovely choice for the covers.*

LEFT, ABOVE *Panels of sheer fabric, with softly gathered pelmets above, diffuse the light and bring an ethereal quality to this dining room.*

LEFT, BELOW *Layering cloth upon cloth, mixing plains, patterns and different colours is an effective way of introducing an interesting table dressing.*

RIGHT *A close-up of this patchwork cloth shows the intricacy of its pattern – a real heirloom.*

fabrics

It is hard to overestimate the importance of fabric in a dining room, where fluid, draping textures are vital in creating an intimate and relaxing atmosphere and to counterpoint the hard surfaces of tables, chairs, crockery and cutlery. Fabric in appealing colours and patterns will bring interest and comfort, while touches such as ribbon ties or appliqué add a delightfully thoughtful and personal element.

Your tablecloth will often be a focal point, and the fabric and style you choose for it will help set the tone for the whole room. A bright floral, large or small checks, or a patchwork of co-ordinating patterns would all be pretty; plain colours could be given a country-style twist with the addition of a ruched edging, a trim made from ricrac or ribbon, or some appliquéd motifs. If you prefer not to use a tablecloth, you can create an interesting display with a long, narrow runner laid along the centre of the table. Place mats and napkins will add to the pretty effect – they could be made from remnants of patterned fabric, or in a plain fabric embellished

with beads, buttons, ribbons, embroidery or appliqué. Pick a consistent colour theme, but mix and match pattern with pattern, and pattern with plain for an individual overall look.

Another key choice is fabric for the window dressings: perhaps a panel of pale, floaty voile with a gathered pelmet, a jolly cotton check curtain with tab tops, or a heavy expanse of dark velvet. Alternatively, a Roman blind made from an informal fabric such as linen or denim can look beautiful. Again, trims, gathered edgings, ruffles, patchwork and appliqué will all add to the effect.

Most dining chairs will benefit from the addition of a soft cushion pad. Don't try too hard to match this fabric exactly with that of the tablecloth – an eclectic combination is far more appropriate to country style, provided the colours complement each other and the patterns don't clash. This is your opportunity to use up

fabric remnants in imaginative ways – even old tea towels (as long as they're not threadbare) could be given a new lease of life, while very small pieces could be made up as a length of patchwork and then sewn together. Chairs that don't quite work in the scheme, or that are badly in need of freshening up, can be transformed with a loose cover, in either a plain cotton or calico, or made from a patterned fabric that adds a spot of lively colour without great expense.

CLOCKWISE, FROM LEFT *A simple blind in a neutral colour can be given extra interest with a decorative border, an unusual pull or – as here – a tie-top.*

Bright seat pads introduce comfort and colour into an otherwise rather austere, all-white room.

Layering one fabric on top of another can have interesting results. Here, a long, thin runner with a pretty pattern has been placed on top of a plain tablecloth.

For the epitome of simplicity, use a white or cream tablecloth with curtains in the same fabric – you can prevent them from looking too plain by ensuring that they are generously gathered.

For a really pretty, country effect, line a cupboard door with gathered panels of gingham.

A pleasant mix of informal fabrics in typically country-style colours and patterns makes this dining area laid-back and inviting.

PROJECT 5

floral tablecloth

Making this tablecloth is a practical and delightful way to use up remnants of chintz, gingham and other printed furnishing fabrics. It is made from four pieced triangles which create a pattern of concentric squares. Although the selection of fabrics in this example might appear random, it is carefully limited to three main colours – pink, blue and cream – which gives cohesion and unity to the overall design.

MATERIALS & EQUIPMENT

selection of furnishing fabric

white sewing thread

squared pattern paper

pencil • long ruler

cutting-out scissors

tailor's chalk

tacking thread • needle

sewing machine

MAKING THE TEMPLATE

1 Mark out a triangle on the pattern paper. Draw a baseline 150 cm (60 in) long, mark the midpoint and draw a 75 cm (30 in) line at right angles. Add two lines joining the ends of the baseline to the top of the shorter line (see below), then cut out the template.

MAKING UP THE TRIANGLES

2 Cut four strips of fabric measuring 10 x 150 cm (4 x 60 in) each. These will form the border of the tablecloth. Fold each strip in half widthways and mark the centre with tailor's chalk. Cut four strips measuring 10 x 134 cm (4 x 52 in) from contrasting fabric to make the next round. Mark the midpoints.

3 With right sides facing, pin and tack one long and one shorter strip together, matching the chalk marks (see step 2). Machine-stitch 1 cm ($\frac{1}{2}$ in) from the edge, then neaten the raw edges with an overlock stitch or zigzag. Press the seam allowance towards the longer strip. Join the other strips in pairs, in the same way.

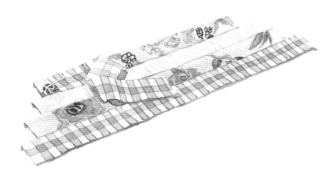

4 The next four strips are 10 x 118 cm (4 x 46 in). Cut out, mark the centres and sew to the previous strips as before. Continue adding strips of fabric (see steps 2 and 3), reducing the length each time by 16 cm (6 in), until each triangle is complete, with ten stripes. You can vary the width of the strips slightly to give variety.

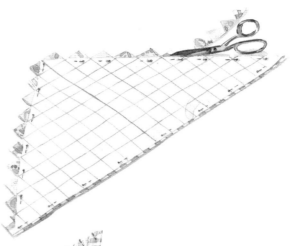

JOINING THE TRIANGLES

5 Pin the paper template to a finished triangle, lining up the long edges, and cut out the fabric (see step 2). Cut out the other three pieces in the same way.

6 With right sides facing, pin two triangles together along one short edge, carefully matching up the seams. Tack and machine-stitch, leaving a 1 cm (½ in) seam allowance. Neaten the raw edges and press the seam to one side. Join the other two triangles in the same way.

7 Pin the two large triangles along the longest edge to make up the square. Tack, machine-stitch, neaten the seam, then press the allowance flat (see left).

FINISHING OFF

8 To finish off the edge, press under a 1 cm (½ in) hem around the border, then press the border in half so that the folded edge lines up with the first seam.

9 Neaten each corner with a mitre. Unfold the deeper turning and fold the corner over at an angle of 45° so that the creases line up to form a right angle.

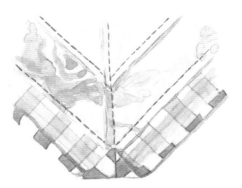

10 Refold the turnings, press lightly and pin the fold to the wrong side, so that it conceals the first seam allowance. Tack in place, then slip-stitch the two sides of each mitre together, starting at

the point and working inwards. Hand stitch the hem to the cloth, sewing through the seam allowance so that the stitches do not show through on the right side. Press the hem.

Dining tables, sideboards, dressers or cabinets are all the most fantastic surfaces on which to make a stunning display of pretty and practical accessories. It could be utterly simple – a jug of fresh flowers or a bowl of pine cones placed in the centre of the table, for example – or slightly more formal, such as a neat row of herbs or spring bulbs in a variety of planters. Or it could be lavish – a profusion of flowers, fruit, vegetables or preserves, shown off in the prettiest of ceramic, enamel, glass, wood or wirework containers.

When setting the table, there are lots of lovely ways to create an informal, attractive scene. Perhaps a small sprig of herbs or leaves, held together with a twist of string and placed on a dinner plate, or a place card in hand-made paper with elegant calligraphy. Or, for a sweetly pretty effect, you could attach a silk flower to a napkin ring with wire, or even sprinkle dried rose petals over the entire table.

finishing touches

OPPOSITE, ABOVE LEFT *Fruit and vegetables make a glorious display in their own right – there's no need to think too carefully about how to set them out.*

OPPOSITE, ABOVE RIGHT *Spring bulbs in assorted pretty planters are a gorgeous centrepiece in this informal country kitchen.*

OPPOSITE, BELOW LEFT *Placing a sprig of lavender on a folded napkin is an appealing finishing touch for a table setting.*

OPPOSITE, BELOW RIGHT *All sorts of containers can be used for attractive displays in the dining room, from ceramic or glass to wood or wirework.*

ABOVE *One of the key ideas in country style is to create a feeling of abundance, and this bowl, which is burgeoning with foliage, is just right.*

LEFT *These patchwork place mats are simply delightful, and the beaded milk-jug cover is a lovely old-fashioned touch.*

PROJECT 6

hop centrepiece

Hops are evocative of the countryside at harvest time, so they are the obvious choice for any arrangement made to celebrate this time of year. This attractive rustic display is surprisingly simple to make – all you need for the basic structure are a sturdy metal ring and four large pillar candles. Natural sisal rope is used to tie the ring to the outside of the candles that support it, providing a frame onto which the textural fresh hops can be bound with wire.

MATERIALS & EQUIPMENT

4 candles, 20 x 10 cm
(8 x 4 in) diameter

1 metal ring wreath frame, 38 cm
(15 in) diameter

6 m (6 yd) sisal rope, 5 mm
(¼ in) diameter

1 vine hops (*Humulus lupulus*),
for approximately 70 sprigs,
20 cm (8 in) long

florist's scissors • fine-gauge gold wire

wire cutters

1 Once complete, this candle arrangement will be difficult to move around, so either assemble it in situ or on a small tray or wooden board. Lay the metal ring flat on your surface and stand the four candles inside it, evenly spaced apart.

2 Cut the sisal rope into four lengths of 150 cm (60 in). Wind one piece four times around one of the candles, roughly 8 cm (3 in) from the base. Put one end of the rope through the metal ring and tie a secure double knot.

3 Use the three remaining lengths of rope to attach the ring to the other three candles in the same way, so that the metal ring is suspended about 8 cm (3 in) above the surface.

4 Cut the hops into approximately 70 sprigs, 20 cm (8 in) long. Lay the first sprig along the ring and bind the stalk to it with gold wire.

5 Gradually build up the decoration by adding more sprigs of hops to the ring, overlapping them and binding them in place with gold wire as before, until the metal ring is completely hidden.

6 Finally, cut some short stems of hops and push the stalks directly into the arrangement. Make sure to fill any gaps and conceal any visible wire.

The kitchen is the focal point of every country-style home, providing not just a practical place for cooking but also a welcoming space for family to gather, for children to play or do homework, for doing laundry, watching television or just chatting to friends. Get the basics right – good appliances sited in convenient positions, tough flooring and plenty of work space – and you can have fun with the rest.

kitchens

Storage, for example, need not be rows of boring fitted cupboards, but could consist of a large pine dresser, supplemented by open shelves, hanging racks, assorted cupboards and chests and wicker baskets. Install concealed lighting to work by and add atmospheric wall lights and chandeliers for decorative effect, and finish off with pretty paint colours and country-style accessories.

CLOCKWISE, FROM TOP LEFT
Open storage can be a really effective way to introduce a country look to your kitchen; just make sure you're prepared to keep it relatively tidy, or else add a few cupboards in which to hide your messy stuff. A rise-and-fall pendant is useful over a large work surface and has a homely, traditional look. Wicker baskets of all shapes and sizes provide handy storage and bring a rustic look to the kitchen. A cheap alternative to fitted cupboard fronts – a simple panel of fabric (in whatever colour or pattern suits your room) threaded over a wire or slender pole. Warm terracotta flagstones set the scene in this appealing room, while a combination of fitted cupboards and open shelving is both practical and attractive.

ABOVE *It's easy to give painted furniture an aged, distressed appearance. Simply rub the corners and edges unevenly with a wax candle, then cover with a coat of paint – the waxed areas will retain their original surface and the over-all effect will be nicely worn.*

RIGHT *Using a strong colour gives a kitchen a very definite personality – and in this room not only the walls are painted red, but also the tongue and groove ceiling and the woodwork around the windows.*

colours & textures

A country-style kitchen is the heart of the home, the centre of family life, and in this room a sense of warmth, comfort, intimacy and easy relaxation is essential. Colour can be quite strong – anything from buttercup yellow to tomato red. Blues or greens can also look gorgeous, while cream is a traditional choice for those who prefer more subtle shades. White combined with another colour, such as lemon yellow or cornflower blue, is another pretty option, and don't forget that you can keep background colours plain and still add a great deal of vitality in the form of accessories such as gleaming copper pots and pans, blue and white china or brightly coloured glassware.

ABOVE *You can pick up informal, country-style kitchenware really cheaply in junk shops, jumble sales and auctions. Choose pieces that are complementary in shape and shade, and create a pretty display on a shelf or flat surface. If you come across a beaten-up old cupboard, too, it is often possible to transform it by painting it, changing the knobs or handles, and perhaps even replacing the door panels with chicken wire or fabric.*

LEFT *Whether it's mugs, bread crocks, saucepans or soup spoons, you can make a display of practically any kitchen equipment. A neat row of identical – or near identical – objects on a shelf or tabletop always looks good.*

LEFT *A stone floor is a beautiful base for a country kitchen, utterly traditional and full of character. This one is made up of randomly sized flags, which adds to its impact.*

ABOVE, LEFT *White and soft blue makes an appealing combination, with no need for any further embellishment.*

ABOVE *Another version of a blue and white kitchen, with plain wooden furniture and simple checked fabric used in gathered panels to line the cupboard doors.*

OPPOSITE, ABOVE *The intricate patterns and vibrant colour of these striking tiles is all that is needed to make a dramatic impact in this otherwise very simple kitchen. By scouring junk shops and reclamation yards you may be able to put together a collection of mismatching (but nevertheless co-ordinating) tiles which could be used in a similar way.*

OPPOSITE, BELOW *Create an eclectic and appealing combination of textures by using natural materials such as wood, wicker, stone, slate, glass, ceramics and metal. Wicker baskets such as these are a nicely informal way to contain assorted items neatly on shelves without enclosing them behind closed doors.*

To start with, a quick coat of emulsion on the walls will go
a long way towards establishing the right atmosphere.
Choose paint with a high proportion of pigment for an
intense effect, or else a chalky surface texture for a softer,
more historic look. The colour and texture of your cupboard
fronts will make as big an impact as those of the walls, and
it is important to get them right. Modern units with their
man-made, smooth, glossy finishes are simply inappropriate,
but there are many ways to disguise them. Use cupboard
paint as a primer and then add colour in the form of an
eggshell top coat. To break up its solid effect you could
use a paint technique such as colourwashing, distressing,
ragging, dragging or spongeing – they would all create
a charming, authentic look and introduce a nicely worn
surface texture. Apply the same techniques to give new
life to old wooden furniture, too, from dressers and tables
to chairs and cupboards. To complete the effect, appliances,
radiators and even tiled splashbacks can be transformed
with a careful application of specialist paint.

PROJECT 7

plate rack

If you are a little bit handy with a saw and hammer, you'll enjoy making this Swedish-style plate rack. It would traditionally have been used to display the family's finest crockery, but will look equally pretty stacked with a few charmingly mismatched plain and printed plates. You can finish it in any way you like to complement your kitchen.

MATERIALS & EQUIPMENT

enough 19 x 150 cm (7½ x 60 in) reclaimed wood, such as floorboarding, or softwood to cut the following pieces:

2 85.5 cm (33 in) lengths, for sides
1 60 cm (24 in) length, for bottom shelf

19 x 50 cm (7½ x 20 in) reclaimed wood or softwood, cut as follows:

3 60 cm (24 in) lengths, for shelves

12.5 x 25 mm (½ x 1 in) softwood, cut as follows:

4 63.8 cm (24 in) lengths, for rails

1 60 cm (24 in) length, for bottom rail

tracing paper • pencil • G-cramps

coping saw or jigsaw

medium and fine sandpaper

wood glue • panel pins • hammer

try square or spirit level • wire wool

4 wall attachments (with screws)

screwdriver

1 On a photocopier, enlarge the template (below) for the two sides by 200 per cent. Transfer the shape onto each of the two rectangular side pieces, making sure you mark the shelf positions on the inside faces.

2 With G-cramps, clamp each piece of wood in turn to the edge of a workbench or a sturdy table and cut out the shapes using a coping saw or jigsaw. Sand the sawn curves smooth to remove any jagged edges.

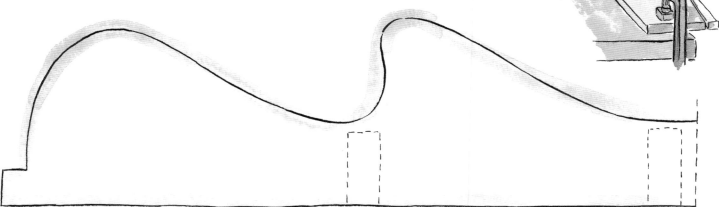

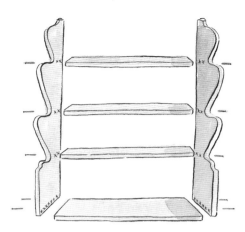

3 The shelves sit between the shaped sides, flush with the straight back edge. Attach them using wood glue and panel pins, inserted from the outside of the side sections. Start with the wider bottom shelf, positioning it level with the bottom edges of the sides. Next, attach the three remaining shelves, lining them up with the marks made in step 1. Use a try square or spirit level to check that they are level and square to the sides.

4 Glue and pin the rails in position. This is done working from the front. Start with the bottom rail, fitting it in between the two sides and flush with the front edge of the bottom shelf to form a step. The other four rails are fitted on the outside edges of the curved sides. Position three of them across each of the widest sections of the top three curves and sit the final one at the very top of the rack, tucking it behind the highest curve.

5 The position of both shelves and rails can be adjusted to fit any size of plate so that you can have smaller plates on the higher shelves, for example. Simply raise or lower them to a suitable height to house your display.

6 To finish the wood, paint or wax to suit your decor. Rub the rack all over with sandpaper and fine-grade wire wool to achieve a smooth surface.

TEMPLATE
Enlarge the template by 200 per cent on a photocopier and cut out the shape twice.

Side (cut 2)

fabrics

Fabrics play an important role in a country-style kitchen, introducing an essential element of softness, texture, colour and pattern. These are unfussy fabrics, however – whatever you choose may be as pretty as a picture, but should also be workmanlike, durable and unpretentious. Cotton, linen, canvas, ticking and denim are all good choices, while muslin can work well for screening windows and wipe-able oilcloth is ideal for covering tables – especially ones that regularly play host to children's painting or sticking sessions. As a starting point, choose colours that complement your overall scheme – you can't go wrong with sunny yellow, bright red, mid blue, soft green, white or cream – and patterns that have stood the test of time, such as checks, ginghams, spriggy florals or simple stripes.

When designing window treatments, you must avoid hanging flapping curtains anywhere near a cooker or hob, and these are best kept away from sinks, too. Instead, opt for a neat little blind which won't dangle in the way. If you make it in a cheerful

ABOVE *These pretty curtains are gathered over a slim pole. Their jolly colours are a lively embellishment to the room.*

BELOW, LEFT *Here, a cupboard with plain glass doors has been given a pretty decorative treatment with the addition of panels of broad-striped fabric attached to the inside.*

BELOW, RIGHT *Don't forget that even the humblest of tea towels can make an attractive addition to your scheme, while an old chair can be disguised with a throw made from a comfortable old blanket.*

OPPOSITE, CLOCKWISE FROM BOTTOM RIGHT *Simple fabric*

has been used for a pretty tablecloth in a kitchen-diner. Make a café curtain from a small remnant of fabric – even a tea towel. Add tab tops or ties and thread over a metal or bamboo pole. These diaphanous curtains are ultra-plain, except for the pretty gathered valance with a cheeky red trim. Casual fabrics look great in a kitchen, and for this simple curtain two remnants have been stitched together and jazzed up with the addition of some appliquéd flowers. Tiny patches of assorted fabrics have been used to create this fabulously eccentric tea cosy.

BELOW, LEFT *This ruched red blind is a good idea behind a sink – decorative but not so flouncy that it will get wet.*

BELOW, RIGHT *A simple, pointed edging adds a lovely, country-style feel to a plain shelf. The matching tea towels below are another nice touch.*

OPPOSITE, ABOVE *An utterly simple solution to the problem of hiding things you don't want seen, without spending*

too much money – a gathered panel of plain fabric hung in front of open shelves.

OPPOSITE, BELOW, FROM LEFT TO RIGHT *Fabric-covered notebooks can be made by hand by covering ready-made books with remnants of linen or cotton, adding a monogrammed patch and some pretty ties. They can be used for recipes, dinner-party notes or just*

plain shopping lists. Use tiny scraps of fabric to cover the lids of jam jars – gingham is traditional, but plains can look equally attractive. There's no reason why oven mitts should be plain and boring. If you can't find a pretty pair in the shops, you could make some yourself, using tough, thick fabric and plenty of wadding inside as heat-proofing.

floral, it will still be perky and pretty. Alternatively, add some interest with a patterned border, a scalloped bottom edge or a ruched pelmet above. At windows or doors that are free from obstruction you can go to town with generous lengths of fabric that will add immense country charm.

Gathered panels of fabric also make a pleasantly informal alternative to the conventional cupboard door. Simply hang from an elasticated wire or a slender pole in front of open shelves to screen whatever is on them. You can use fabric to line cupboard doors and to edge the fronts of shelves, too.

For a fun, personal touch make accessories such as egg cosies, tea cosies or jam jar covers from whatever bits of fabric you can lay your hands on; you may also want to hang a cross-stitch sampler on a wall as a pretty adornment.

And, finally, there are the fabrics without which a kitchen simply would not function – tea towels and oven gloves. These are essentially utilitarian, and as such must be practical and fit for their jobs, but that's no reason why they can't also be attractive in themselves, in patterns and colours that complement and enhance the overall look and feel of the room.

MATERIALS & EQUIPMENT

3 different main fabrics

lining fabric

1.5 cm (⅝ in) wide red braid

yellow-checked curtains

These cheerful curtains are guaranteed to bring a relaxed, sunny atmosphere to any room. They use panels of three co-ordinating fabrics joined horizontally, with vivid scarlet braid sewn over the seams to conceal the joins. The bold checks and trim have a pleasing, rustic simplicity that is echoed by the simple ties that hold the curtains to an iron pole.

1 Measure the window to calculate fabric quantities (see page 104). Each panel occupies one third of the drop of the finished curtain. Add 1.5 cm (⅝ in) to each panel for each seam. Add 8 cm (3 in) to the top panel for the heading and 16 cm (6½ in) to the bottom panel for the hem. Each curtain must be the width of the pole plus 12 cm (5 in) for side hems. The lining must be 4 cm (1¾ in) smaller than the finished curtain all round. Cut out the fabric.

2 Place the top panel on a flat surface with the middle panel on top, right sides together and raw edges aligned. Pin, baste and machine stitch the two panels together, using a 1.5 cm (⅝ in) seam allowance and matching up the checks as best you can. Press open the seam. Attach the bottom panel to the middle panel in the same way.

3 Cut two strips of braid to the width of the curtain. Centre the braid over the seams between the panels on the right side of the curtain. Pin, baste and machine-stitch down both edges of the braid.

4 Press in a 6 cm (2½ in) hem at each side of the curtain and a double 8 cm (3 in) hem at the bottom. Press in the angled mitres (see page 105). Pin and baste the hems in place. Herringbone-stitch the side hems. Slip-stitch the base hem and the mitres.

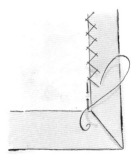

5 Cut out the lining. Press in a 2 cm (¾ in) hem along each side edge and a 2 cm (¾ in) double base hem. Pin and baste the hems. Mitre the corners (see page 105) and machine-stitch the hems in place.

6 Place the curtain on a flat surface, wrong side up. Place the lining on top, right side up. Match up the corners of the lining with the mitred corners of the curtain and align the top raw edges. Pin the curtain and lining together along the top raw edges. Pin and baste the lining to the curtain. Slip-stitch the lining to the curtain fabric. Leave the bottom of the lining open, as the curtain will hang better.

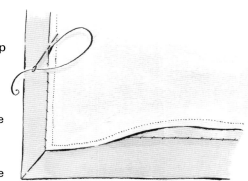

7 The number of ties needed will depend on the width of the curtain. There should be one tie every 25 cm (10 in). Cut a strip of fabric 6 x 50 cm (2½ x 20 in) for each tie. Make up the ties (see page 105) knotting the ends of each one.

8 Lay the curtain flat, right side up. Using fabric pen, lightly mark a line 8 cm (3 in) below the top raw edge. Place a tie at each top corner of the curtain and space the other ties at 25 cm (10 in) intervals in between. Pin and baste the halfway point of each tie to the marked line, then machine-stitch all the way along the line, taking in the ties as you go.

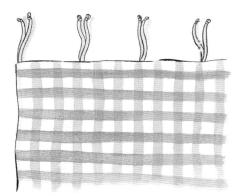

9 Press in a double 4 cm (1¾ in) fold to the wrong side along the top edges of the curtain. Pin, baste and slip-stitch the folded edge of the curtain to the lining.

10 Working at the two top corners of the curtain, slip-stitch the open ends of the top hem together. Press the finished curtains, then tie them to the pole with loose bows.

LEFT *Large wicker baskets make useful storage and can be tucked away neatly under a table, as here. They are also delightfully traditional and add country charm to any kitchen.*

BELOW, LEFT *Painted mugs can be used as decorative accessories as well as for cups of tea.*

BELOW, RIGHT *Even plain kitchen utensils can be turned into a beautiful display – these wooden spoons and spatulas are easily accessible for a busy cook, but look great popped into a row of matching white pots.*

OPPOSITE, ABOVE LEFT *This pretty pitcher has been put to good use as a holder for kitchen implements. The tiles in the background are casually mismatching but terribly pretty.*

OPPOSITE, ABOVE RIGHT *Use a mantelpiece, windowsill or other flat surface to display stoneware, glassware or other attractive kitchen necessities.*

OPPOSITE, BELOW *Country style is unforced and understated, but with the right mix of useful and attractive objects – just easy-going, simple and traditional – you will naturally arrive at the right look.*

finishing touches

Whatever colours, textures and fabrics you have used to create the backbone of your kitchen scheme, it is the finishing touches that will pull everything together and give the room real heart and soul. Not all finishing touches are last-minute accessories, however – here you will find that practical, everyday items can not only be useful for cooking but also for creating charming and informal displays that really add to the overall atmosphere.

If you have wall-to-wall, floor-to-ceiling fitted cupboards, it is worth considering removing one or two and replacing them with some open shelves. You may even be lucky enough to have a traditional dresser, a butcher's block, a mantel-piece or a spacious windowsill – you simply need a surface on which you can casually arrange potted herbs, antique glasses, stoneware jugs, chintz-printed crockery or the like. From hooks, peg rails or metal bars you can hang pans, implements, tea towels, chopping boards and so on, while on the floor you can stack baskets and boxes.

Although the essence of country style is an unplanned, unforced look, it is still worth considering how you can arrange things so that they are shown to their best advantage. Shiny modern appliances are, ideally, kept behind closed doors, as are unexciting tins of food, plastic lidded boxes and anything else that either offers little visual interest or is just plain unattractive. Then group together items that are good-looking singly or en masse – a wooden spoon, for example, might be boring on its own, but could look great popped into a jug with several others and stood beside the hob or on a nearby shelf. Rows of white plates could be stacked on shelves, interspersed with coloured crockery or vases of flowers, while coloured tea towels could be hung from a Shaker-style peg rail. Even utilitarian objects such as cheese graters, bread boards, colanders or soup ladles, as long as they're not too sleek and modern in style, can become delightful decorative accessories when displayed in a way that is usable but that also emphasizes their inherent charm.

ABOVE, LEFT AND RIGHT *The owner of this house has created a dresser-cum-worksurface from what is in fact simply a small table with some shelving above. She has used an all-white scheme which contrasts beautifully with the warm old wood, while the natural colours of foliage, fruit and vegetables add a dash of vibrancy.*

OPPOSITE, ABOVE *A Shaker-style peg rail is a practical way to store often-used items close to hand, while at the same time showing off their interesting shapes, colours and textures.*

OPPOSITE, BELOW, FROM LEFT TO RIGHT *Simplicity itself: a chopping board with a heart shape cut out so that it can be hung easily. These wire implements are unlikely to be used very often but their graphic shapes make a fantastic display against the weathered wooden wall. On a sunny windowledge you can't beat a sweet display of herbs in mismatching but pretty pots.*

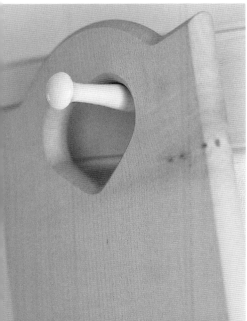
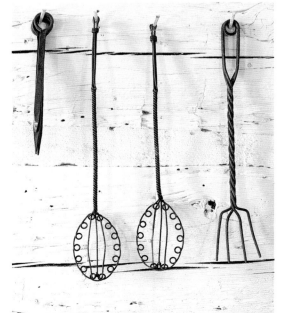

PROJECT 9

key cupboard

Finding keys can become a permanent pastime, unless you always return them to the same place. Keep them all in this shallow cupboard, which could hang on the wall, and you will never need to search for them again. If you have the wood cut to size by your supplier, the rest of the project is straightforward. The key design on the door can be painted freehand or with a stencil, using watered-down emulsion.

MATERIALS & EQUIPMENT

12.5 mm (½ in) softwood, cut as follows:
2 240 x 55 mm (9½ x 2 in), for sides
2 203 x 70 mm (8 x 2¾ in), for base
and top

6 mm (¼ in) softwood, cut as follows:
2 240 x 25 mm (9½ x 1 in), for door
frame sides
2 110 x 25 mm (4½ x 1 in), for door
frame top and bottom

6 mm (¼ in) plywood, cut as follows:
1 240 x 185 mm (9½ x 7¼ in), for back

1 240 x 160 mm (9½ x 6¼ in), for door
panel

small strip of wood, 43 mm (1¾ in)
length, for door stop

small door knob (with screw)

wood glue • panel pins • hammer

medium and fine sandpaper • bradawl

screwdriver • 2 butt hinges
(with screws)

8 cup hooks (with screws) for keys

hand drill with 4 mm (⅙ in) screw bit

1 Butt the edges of the side panels up to the back piece and glue as shown. Reinforce with panel pins knocked in from the back.

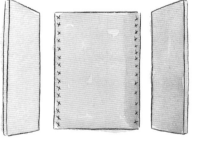

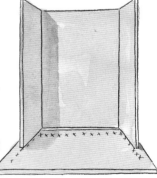

2 Apply glue to the underside of the assembled back and sides and attach them to the base. Position the base so that one long edge is flush with the back of the side panels, leaving an equal 9 mm (⅓ in) overhang at both sides.

3 Apply glue to the top of the assembled cupboard and position the top section so that it corresponds exactly with the base – flush with the back and with a 9 mm (⅓ in) overlap around the front and sides. Smooth all edges with medium then fine sandpaper.

5 Apply glue to the plywood door, as shown, then lie the assembled frame on top. Press together until the glue has bonded. Smooth the joined edges with sandpaper.

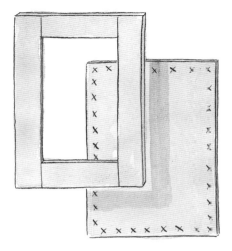

4 To make the door, assemble the frame pieces as shown, apply glue and butt the pieces together.

6 Next, attach the door knob; the one used here has a diameter of 22 mm ($^7/_8$ in). Make a pilot hole for the knob, using a bradawl, and screw it in place halfway down the right-hand frame.

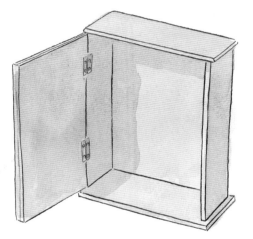

7 Position the hinges on the inside of the door as shown. Make pilot holes for the screws with a bradawl and screw in position. Check that the door closes properly without rubbing. Adjust the tightness of the screws if necessary. To make sure the door hangs evenly.

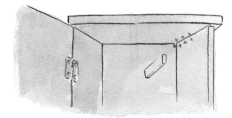

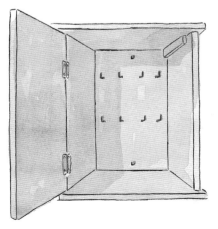

9 Using a bradawl, make pilot holes for the hooks. Position the hooks in two neat rows of four, with a gap in between to allow the keys to hang down. Screw the hooks in place. Mark two more holes through the entire thickness of the wood at the top and bottom of the rear panel for securing the cupboard to a wall. Use a hand drill fitted with a 4 mm ($^1/_6$ in) screw bit to drill the holes.

8 Stick a small piece of wood to the top inside of the right-hand panel, 12 mm ($^1/_2$ in) in from the front, so that the door will close to the correct position.

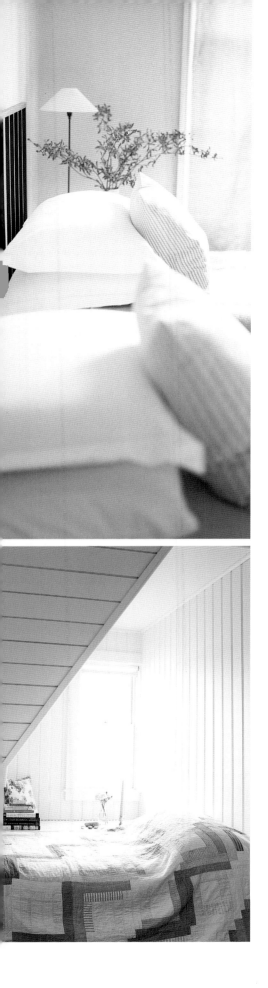

In a country-style bedroom, the emphasis is on creating a calm and pretty space which is as cosy for reading a book or watching television as it is conducive to a good night's sleep. Of course, a comfortable bed is the number-one priority, whether it is a four-poster, a curly-metal affair, a sleigh bed or a plain divan. On the floor, many people like the feel of a soft carpet, although wooden floorboards with a few

bedrooms

rugs scattered about look lovely, too. Walls might be painted in soft, gentle colours to create a restful atmosphere, though darker shades, if you prefer them, can be warm and intimate. Storage is vital to avoid clutter – a capacious wardrobe and a simple chest of drawers should suffice, and soft furnishings provide the vital finishing touches, from curtains and bed canopies to bedcovers, quilts and cushions.

CLOCKWISE, FROM CENTRE: *Lace, frills, ribbons and embroidery are all ideal to use as accessories in a very feminine, country-style bedroom. Creamy walls are the ideal background for a mix of fabrics in a variety of patterns. The austerity of this monochrome room, with dark metal bedsteads and white linen, is offset by the vibrant flowers beside the bed. The bold design of a patchwork quilt (relatively* *straightforward to make yourself) can be the focal point in an otherwise plain room. Intricate timber rafters in this attic bedroom create such an interesting pattern and, with the floorboards, a homely texture, that the rest of the decoration has been kept utterly simple. This room is pared down to the minimum, but all the essentials are there, and its strong colours and patterns add richness and vivacity.*

colours & textures

A country-style bedroom is the ultimate in comfort, while also
being full of charm and character. The laid-back, low-key nature of
this look means that a sense of relaxation and intimacy is easy to
achieve, especially with the right choice of colours and a good
mix of textures.

Soft creams and pastels are ideal for paintwork on the walls:
use a chalky, matt emulsion for a lovely effect, and either leave
woodwork bare (stripped pine, rich mahogany or waxed oak all
look great) or cover with satin gloss in a co-ordinating colour.
If you prefer wallpaper, pretty floral patterns – on a relatively small
scale and, again, in faded colours – is ideal. You could even
combine one papered wall with paintwork elsewhere. For those
who prefer their colours stronger and richer, choose deep reds,
purples or blues, but avoid anything too harsh and bright: there's

OPPOSITE, ABOVE *A blue and white colour scheme is unfussy and timeless, with masses of country charm. The unsophisticated nature of the striped cotton bedlinen has utilitarian appeal.*

OPPOSITE, BELOW *This is a warm, mustardy yellow that is neither too insipid nor too strong. It works well with the plain wooden furniture.*

ABOVE *Create interest in a bedroom by combining plain paintwork with one feature wall, whether it's covered in wallpaper or stencilled with a simple, pretty pattern. In this room the plaster walls have a fabulously rough, intriguing texture, while the armchair is delightfully shabby.*

ABOVE RIGHT *An old, inexpensive cupboard can be transformed with a coat of paint and turned into an attractive feature of a bedroom – like this sweet bedside cabinet. The bed ends were made from two pieces of medium-density fibreboard that were cut into shape and hammered onto a broken bed.*

RIGHT *The bright-yellow walls of this bedroom are combined with fabrics in white, blue, pink and green, including several different floral patterns and a checked blanket. It all blends into a fresh, eclectic, happy whole.*

LEFT *The natural colour and texture of untreated wood is predominant in this informal room. Thick, soft bedding makes a nice contrast and creates a homely, inviting feel.*

ABOVE, **LEFT** *It's easy to add spots of colour to an otherwise plain bedroom, simply by introducing a vivacious curtain, lamp, bedcover or even a vase of flowers.*

ABOVE, **RIGHT** *The serenity of this light-filled eyrie is undisturbed – nothing but wood, white paint and white linens.*

OPPOSITE, **TOP** *There is a variety of textures in this bedroom – from the thick curtain to the rough mirror frame, the wicker chair to the padded quilt – which bring subtle, sensual appeal.*

OPPOSITE, **CENTRE** *Strong colours in the bedroom aren't for everyone, but if used carefully they can be wonderfully warm, cheerful and inviting.*

OPPOSITE, **BOTTOM** *Smooth, plain, white bedlinen contrasts superbly with rough planked walls in this rustic-meets-luxury country retreat.*

a fine line between warmth and brashness. Elsewhere in the room, flooring (whether carpets or wooden boards plus rugs), furniture and fabrics should work with your basic scheme, but don't worry too much about making everything match perfectly – a mixture of colours has just the right casual and eclectic feel. Alternatively, go for simplicity by teaming white or off-white with just one other colour – perhaps blue, lemon yellow or rosy pink.

Finally, this is the place to experiment with junk-shop finds that you can easily transform with a lick of paint or some fabric cheats. Throw an old blanket over a dilapidated chair or make a new cushion pad for a seat, repaint a bedstead, a lamp base or a side table, and try your hand at stencilling a casual pattern across a chair back, on the lid of a blanket box or over a cupboard door. It's surprisingly easy – the results don't have to be ultra-professional just inventive, appealing and attractive to live with.

PROJECT 10
driftwood frame

Wood gnarled and bleached by the sun adds a primitive attraction to any interior, and half the fun of this creation is collecting the driftwood from a park or seashore. The beauty of this arrangement, which is put together on a rigid wire base, is that it is simple and inexpensive to produce, and works well as a unique and eye-catching detail against any backdrop, whether modern or traditional.

MATERIALS & EQUIPMENT

rectangular wire frame,
60 x 45 cm (24 x 18 in)

8 large pieces of driftwood

40 driftwood twigs

1 large, flat pebble

fine-grade sandpaper

reel wire • wire cutters

natural string • scissors

hot glue gun and glue sticks

picture hook (optional)

1 Lay out your pieces of driftwood and the rectangular wire frame on a flat, non-scratch surface. Work out the best way to arrange the wood on the frame; the largest piece will probably look best along the bottom edge. Using fine-grade sandpaper, smooth away any protrusions on the underside of the wood pieces so that they will lie flush with the frame.

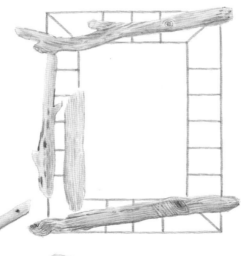

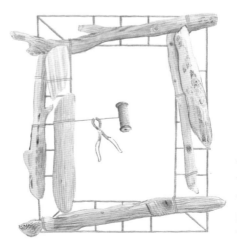

2 Using reel wire, bind each piece of wood securely onto the wire frame and then cut the wire with wire cutters. Fasten the longer pieces of wood at both ends, to hold them in position on the frame.

3 To disguise the sections where wood has been tied onto the frame with reel wire, wind natural string around the wire and fasten it in place with a double knot before cutting it with scissors.

4 Build up the driftwood frame by arranging smaller pieces of wood on top of the main structure. When you are happy that these smaller pieces fill in the gaps, glue them in place on the frame.

5 Finish off the frame by gluing on small twigs. Use them to fill in any gaps between the larger pieces of wood and also to hide areas where the wire frame is still visible.

6 Finally, glue the large pebble onto the bottom left-hand corner of the frame. When the glue is dry, hang the frame on a nail, or tie a loop of reel wire to the frame and hang it from a strong picture hook.

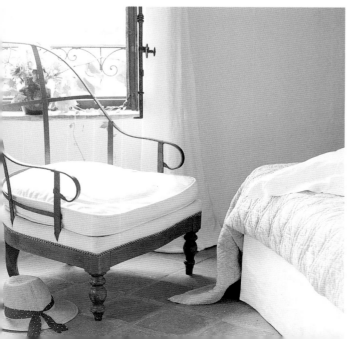

fabrics

A combination of pretty fabrics makes the bedroom a sumptuously romantic, soft and feminine place to be. You can really go to town with bedlinen, bedspreads and covers, throws, pillows, cushions and bolsters, curtains, and accessories such as lavender bags or hot-water-bottle covers. When choosing fabrics, avoid patterns and colours that look too well matched in favour of a casual, eclectic mix. Combine inexpensive new fabrics with pieces picked up in second-hand shops or jumble sales. And, if anything looks too bright and new, soak it in cold tea overnight for an instant ageing effect.

The easiest way to start is with plain white sheets and pillowcases, adding a quilted or patchwork bedspread made from fabric remnants. This can be as simple as large squares or strips sewn together, or as complicated as the traditional American quilts which use a variety of cut-out shapes in complex patterns. Pile on throws (knitted, crocheted, lacy or plain), blankets and bedcovers, layering them in an easy,

OPPOSITE, TOP *Floral fabrics in soft colours are ideal for a bedroom. Here, a quilted bedcover is the focal point, while piles of cushions, in mismatching fabrics, have been added for a relaxed and cosy feel. The window treatment has been made from panels of plain white voile, hung loosely from a painted wooden pole.*

OPPOSITE, CENTRE *Bolsters are easy to make and give a more structured look than squashy cushions.*

OPPOSITE, BOTTOM *A metal chair can be softened by the addition of a plump cushion.*

ABOVE *A soft-toy lavender bag can be tied to a bed frame and makes a delightful accessory.*

LEFT, TOP *Lace, voile, frills, quilting and delicate floral patterns are all ideal for the country-style bedroom. Plain walls and floors ensure that the end result isn't over the top.*

LEFT, CENTRE *Cover a small lidded box with a fabric remnant (glue it carefully, folding the edges in neatly) to make a jewellery box that's both pretty and useful.*

LEFT, BOTTOM *Use fabric generously for this look – here, a gathered valance has been fitted around the base of the bed.*

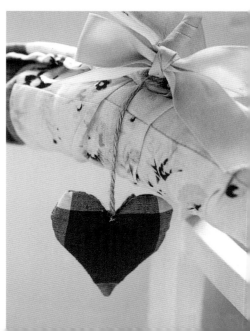

cosy way. Plenty of cushions and bolsters add atmosphere – make your own, using a mix of fabrics and trimming them with gathered edgings. Do the same for comfortable cushion pads and pretty loose covers for bedside seating. Window treatments should be simple – either a Roman or roller blind teamed with a fixed drape at either side of the window, or a pair of curtains, generously gathered and perhaps customized with a deep border of a different fabric, a contrast lining, or a trimming of ribbon or ricrac. Tabs or tie tops make an attractive, informal alternative to the usual curtain heading, though they can be slightly more awkward to draw.

If you need privacy during the day, pin up a panel of muslin or gather a length of lace or sheer fabric over a slim wooden pole. Finish off with accessories made from left-over scraps of fabric – anything from heart-shaped lavender bags and knitted hot-water-bottle covers to fabric-covered jewellery boxes and padded clothes hangers.

OPPOSITE, ABOVE *When mixing patterns it's important to ensure that the colours you choose co-ordinate really well. The patchwork bedcover, gingham cushion and bolster and checked curtains here are all in a cheerful mid-red that is exactly right for this look.*

OPPOSITE, BELOW, FROM LEFT TO RIGHT *You can never have too many old-fashioned quilts, their faded colours and spriggy patterns a perfect embodiment of the best of country style. Florals and checks in the same colour are both ideal fabrics for this look, and together they create a relaxed and appealing combination. Small scraps of fabric can be put to good use and turned into gorgeous accessories, such as this padded clothes hanger.*

ABOVE, LEFT *Layering fabrics is really effective – here, the owner has put valances with bedcovers, plus blankets, throws and pillows.*

ABOVE, RIGHT *Toile de Jouy fabric, with its distinctive monochrome illustrations, is rather a grand fabric for this look, but this bedcover is softly comfortable and teamed with some mismatching cushions and a simple woven rug.*

PROJECT 11

patchwork duvet cover

The key to creating this beautiful duvet cover is to balance the colours – here, a lovely dusty pink combines perfectly with soft lilac, blue and white. Although the sumptuous texture of the damask used here is gorgeous enough in itself, when choosing fabrics look out for details such as monograms, laundry marks or makers' labels, which all make lovely features.

MATERIALS AND EQUIPMENT

selection of laundered damask napkins and tablecloths

white cotton double sheet

2.5 m (100 in) woven tape

matching sewing thread

dressmaker's pins

sewing machine

sewing kit

CUTTING OUT

The instructions are for a double-sized duvet cover. Adjust the measurements accordingly to fit a larger or smaller duvet. Cut the back panel and facing from the sheet so that the existing hems lie along one short edge of the back panel and one long edge of the facing strip.

BACK PANEL

width = 200 cm (80 in)

length = 230 cm (92 in)

FACING

width = 5 cm (2 in)

length = 200 cm (80 in)

1 To make the front panel, trim off the hems and cut away any damaged areas from the napkins and tablecloths, to give a selection of strips and rectangles in different sizes. Lay the fabric out on the floor in an approximate 220 cm (88 in) square, taking time to get a good balance of shape and colour within the arrangement.

2 Start by sewing the smaller pieces together, then join them to form larger blocks, until the front is complete. Pin and tack each seam, then stitch 1 cm (½ in) from the edge. Press the seam allowance to one side and top-stitch 3 mm (⅛ in) from the join. Trim the finished panel to 200 cm (80 in) square.

3 Pin and tack the facing strip along the bottom of the front panel so that the right side of the strip is against the wrong side of the panel. Stitch together along the bottom edge, 1 cm (½ in) from the edge, then press the facing to the right side. Pin in place, then stitch along the same edge, 5 mm (¼ in) from the seam, then top-stitch the edge of the facing to the cover.

4 Press 30 cm (12 in) along the hemmed edge of the back panel to the wrong side, making a deep turning.

5 With the turning on the outside and right sides facing, pin and tack together the top and sides of the front and back panel together. Machine-stitch 5 mm (¼ in) from the edge, then trim and neaten the seam allowance with a zigzag or overlocking stitch. Turn right side out and press.

6 Pin and tack the front and back panels together for 25 cm (10 in) at either side of the opening and machine stitch close to the edges.

7 Mark the positions of the ties by placing five pins at regular intervals along both edges of the opening.

8 Cut the tape into ten 25 cm (10 in) lengths. Neaten one end of each tie, then press under a narrow turning at the other end. Tack, then hand-stitch each tie securely in place on the inside of the cover.

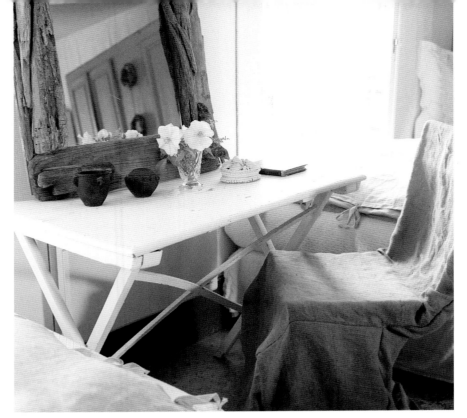

LEFT *A driftwood mirror frame and simple chair cover are inexpensive, yet highly effective in creating a casual country look.*

BELOW *Just a simple flower in any sort of informal container can add a characterful, fresh simplicity.*

OPPOSITE, CLOCKWISE FROM TOP LEFT *It's easy to make simple drawstring bags from inexpensive fabrics. Hang them together in a row and they are both pretty and practical. You could use hooks of any sort, perhaps found in a second-hand shop (they don't necessarily have to match), screwed to a length of painted board. Adapt your storage so that it has a quirky individuality – here, an uneven length of bamboo has been attached to the bottom of a shelf to create a delightful hanging space. A slim shelf, whether specially designed or improvised, can be used to display a varied selection of finds, from shells or pebbles to postcards, bud vases or any kind of personal mementoes. For a drawer full of antique linen, the perfect finishing touch is a sprig of lavender.*

finishing touches

Once you've got the basics of the bedroom right, you can enjoy assembling the final elements that bring the room to life. You may wish to add all sorts of personal, individual touches, or simply leave the room quite plain, perhaps with just a jam jar full of flowers picked from the garden for a splash of colour.

For practicality as well as prettiness, choose a mirror with an interesting frame – perhaps gilded, stencilled or made from driftwood – and place it above the dressing table. A lamp beside the bed is essential, but make sure it has character and charm – if necessary, customize it by painting the base or attaching ribbon or beads to the shade. Even such simple things as laundry bags can be turned into an attractive display if made from lovely fabric and hung from a row of peg hooks. And for an appropriately natural, understated look, arrange leaves, feathers, shells or pebbles on tabletops or shelves, where their colours and textures will add subtle decorative effect.

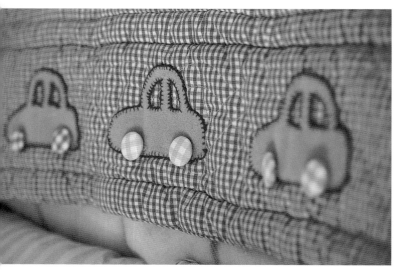

PROJECT 12

child's quilt

Cot quilts are popular gifts for new babies, who can lie on them when very small or be wrapped in them for outings. As the child grows, the quilt takes on a new role as a bedcover or play mat. This charming gingham quilt, with sweet appliquéd car motifs, continues a long-established custom and would undoubtedly make a very well-received present – if you can bear to give it away.

MATERIALS & EQUIPMENT

1 120 x 135 cm (48 x 54 in) rectangle of polyester wadding

2 110 x 125 cm (43 x 50 in) rectangles of red gingham

pair of compasses

thick tracing paper

sharp pencil

blue chalk dressmaker's pencil

long ruler

quilting thread or walking foot attachment for sewing machine

turquoise felt

scraps of blue, green and yellow gingham

skein of red stranded embroidery cotton

6 2.5 cm (1 in) self-cover buttons

matching sewing thread

sewing kit

sewing machine

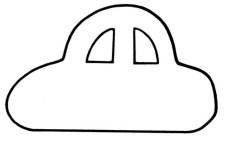

Enlarge templates to 200 per cent

1 Lay the wadding out flat, place the two pieces of gingham, right sides facing, centrally on top of it and smooth them out. Pin, then tack together around all four edges.

2 Machine-stitch 1 cm (½ in) from the edge, leaving a 50 cm (20 in) gap in the centre of one edge. Pin and tack under the seam allowance along either side of the gap. Trim the surplus wadding and clip the corners.

3 Turn right side out through the gap so that the wadding is sandwiched between the two pieces of gingham. Close the gap by hand with small slip stitches and press the seams lightly.

4 Use the compasses to make two quarter-circle templates from thick tracing paper, with diameters of 17 cm and 19 cm (7 in and 7½ in). Enlarge the two heart templates (above) as directed.

5 Use the chalk pencil and ruler to mark a line 3cm (1¼ in) from the four edges. Rule two parallel lines 15 and 18 cm (6 and 7 in) from each long edge and 18 and 21 cm (7 and 8 in) from the short edges.

6 Mark two parallel curves at each inside corner by drawing round the quarter-circle templates with the chalk pencil. Draw round the two hearts, one inside the other, within each corner. Rule and mark a 38 cm (15 in) square in the centre of the quilt and draw four double hearts inside. Still using the chalk pencil, fill in the rest of the space with a diamond grid of parallel lines 3 cm (1¼ in) apart.

7 Starting from the centre, tack the three layers together securely by sewing diagonally out to each corner, then to the centre of each side. Work parallel lines of tacking stitch, approximately 15 cm (6 in) apart, across the whole surface of the quilt.

8 Quilt along all the chalk lines either by hand using quilting thread and a short needle or by machine using a special walking foot so that the quilt does not become puckered. If you wish, you can quilt inside the borders with more parallel or wavy lines and add circular motifs to the corners.

9 Cut out three felt cars following the template (opposite). Pin, then tack them in a row along one short edge of the quilt. Sew in place by hand using blanket stitch (see page 105) worked in all six strands of the embroidery thread. Then stitch through just the top layer of fabric.

10 Cover two buttons in each of the three different-coloured ginghams and stitch them securely in place to represent the cars' wheels.

The key to putting together a successful country-style bathroom is to get the right combination of informal, traditional good looks and practical, functional modern comfort. You can be imaginative with the basic ingredients, as this is a look that's eclectic and individual – but make sure you avoid furnishings that are too sleek, smart, cool and sophisticated-looking. For authentic, old-fashioned appeal, you can't beat the capacious luxury of a roll-top bath, matched with a generously sized washbasin.

bathrooms

Walls might be covered in tongue and groove, patterned ceramic tiles or just a wash of coloured paint, while the floor might be stone, tile, boards or linoleum. Ensure that the room is toasty warm with a cast-iron column radiator or a large heated towel rail, and finish with some free-standing storage.

TOP, LEFT *A traditional roll-top bath, column radiator and high-level cistern create a sense of timeless style, while the quirky plaster roundel above the bath is rather charming.*

TOP, RIGHT *The quiet character of this bathroom comes from its mix of soft colours and unassuming furnishings.*

BOTTOM, LEFT *Natural materials are ideal for every room in a country-style house, but particularly so in a bathroom, where you can really appreciate the tactile nature of warm wood, cool stone and nubbly towelling.*

BOTTOM, CENTRE *Decorated Victorian ceramic tiles make an unusual but effective splashback next to the bath.*

BOTTOM, RIGHT *Rows of wooden shelves are a good way to store and display bathroom accessories.*

colours & textures

Although white is the standard colour for a bathroom suite, there are plenty of ways in which you can introduce the more interesting shades that characterize country style. Walls might be washed with paint or panelled in natural wood, while the areas next to the bath and basin could have jolly, hand-painted tiles as a splashback. Even the floor could be given a few coats of paint, or be covered in patterned ceramic tiles or traditional linoleum. And accessories, from towels to bath oils, can add glorious dashes of colour or intriguing surface textures.

In general, watery blues and greens are ideal choices, though a seaside theme including mid-blue, turquoise, primrose yellow, bright red or bubblegum pink (think of beach huts and deckchairs) will also work nicely for this look. Of course, if you want an all-white bathroom there is nothing wrong with that – provided you include a variety of textures and mix white with naturals, such as wood and wicker, so as to avoid a sterile, modern effect.

ABOVE, FROM LEFT TO RIGHT *For
an all-white bathroom to have
the right rustic feel, it's important
to include some natural wood and
rough, distressed surfaces – such
as this beautifully peeling painted
floor. Tongue and groove boarding
painted in a soft, greyish-blue is
a traditional choice for a
bathroom, especially when
combined with a roll-top bath
with brass 'telephone'-style taps.
Wood-planked walls are a more
down-to-earth alternative to tongue
and groove. The lovely warmth
of natural wood – in this case,
in the form of a sash window and
Shaker-style peg rail – contrasts
wonderfully with the bright, shiny
white of ceramic surfaces.*

LEFT *Here, natural wood has
been used for an unpretentious
vanity unit, with painted wood
for the walls.*

RIGHT *This monochrome scheme
is composed mainly of creamy
whites, with strong black as an
occasional counterpoint.*

LEFT *These sweet gathered curtains are hung from portiere rods either side of a dormer window. They co-ordinate nicely with the hand towel and the bath bag that's perched on the shelf above the washbasin. Notice the understated curtain that's been used as a screen below the basin.*

BELOW, FROM LEFT TO RIGHT *The large drying rack rigged up around this roll-top bath functions perfectly as a shower screen, with a couple of ordinary plastic curtains. This half-curtain is ideal for privacy, yet still allows plenty of light through the top half of the window. Wooden louvre blinds are great for larger bathroom windows, and here the whole effect has been softened with the addition of a ruched blind above.*

OPPOSITE *Blue and white checks liven up a plain white bathroom, in the form of a panel strung across the bottom of the window for privacy and a decorative, shaped pelmet at the top.*

fabrics

Fabric doesn't play as large a part in a bathroom as elsewhere in the house, but it can still make a delightful appearance in the form of blinds, neat little curtains, screens across shelving, laundry bags, bathmats and, of course, towels. What's more, each time you use a length of fabric, it adds a note of softness, fluidity, colour and pattern that combines nicely with the predominantly hard materials elsewhere, such as ceramic and wood. As far as pattern goes, ginghams and other checks are ideal, as are delicate floral patterns, plains or stripes.

When choosing fabrics for window treatments, it's best to concentrate on light cottons, linens and voiles – nothing too heavy that will retain moisture. You could make them up as plain panels with hooks at each end, or gather them over portiere rods or a bamboo pole. Alternatively, a simple roller or Roman blind, perhaps with a shaped bottom edge, is perfect.

finishing touches

Bathroom furnishings have to be extremely practical, but there are plenty of opportunities to have fun with pretty accessories, too. A nautical theme can be really attractive, with sweet little sailing boats arranged on windowsills or shelves, or beside the bath. You could also add model lighthouses and beach huts, antique ship's fittings (such as portholes or bulkhead lamps) and naïve maritime paintings. Alternatively, a natural scheme might incorporate shells, pebbles, driftwood, starfish and sponges. Don't forget storage accessories such as soap dishes and toothbrush holders – they could be made of coloured glass, blue-and-white china or wirework, while free-standing furniture such as rush-seated stools or small, painted cupboards will add to the atmosphere. Mirrors are essential and can easily be embellished to suit your scheme – if you buy one with a plain, broad wooden frame, you could paint it, gild it or cover it with driftwood, shells or mosaic tiles. Finally, for a touch of extra colour and softness, add a home-made rag rug beside the bath and a selection of towels with patterned trimmings.

ABOVE, FROM LEFT TO RIGHT *Soaps don't have to be boring – choose some with pretty colours and shapes, and an irresistible scent, and they become delightful finishing touches. Flowers and foliage cut from the garden can be displayed in an informal container such as a milk bottle or jam jar. Add a delicately patterned fabric trim to white towels and dressing gowns for a really gorgeous country effect.*

OPPOSITE *A row of small hooks makes for inexpensive storage, while junk-shop finds such as metal buckets or little wooden stools can be put to great use in a country-style bathroom. Here, the owner has casually displayed a small model pond yacht as a decorative touch in what is a really charming, understated and inexpensive room.*

practicalities

Most of the projects in this book are quick and easy to make by anyone who enjoys kitchen-table craft. Some, however, require a little more expertise and a few pieces of specialist equipment. Even the most challenging, however, should be enjoyable for anyone who is keen and creative. These practical tips should help you on your way.

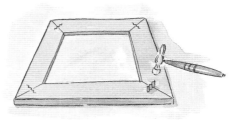

Corrugated fastener

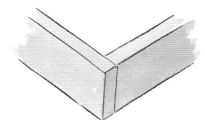

Butt joint

Measuring windows

CORRUGATED FASTENER

Glue the four lengths of wood together to form a flat frame. Clamp the glued corners with mitre clamps and reinforce the joints with corrugated fasteners before removing the clamps.

BUTT JOINT

This involves squaring off the ends to be joined, applying glue to one end grain, then lining it up with the side of the other piece. The joint is usually reinforced by pinning through from the back, but corner blocks can be inserted for extra strength.

ADHESIVE

For simplification, when wood glue is specified in the projects, white wood-working glue is meant. Although it is known by many different trade names it is basically PVA (polyvinyl acetate), a thick water-based adhesive that is transparent when it dries. It is easily applied and sets at room temperature.

Always make sure that the surfaces of wood which are to be fixed fit each other properly and are free from dust. If necessary, smooth them with sandpaper first and then dust them with a soft cloth. Apply enough glue to coat the wood but not so much that it drips and runs – too much glue will weaken the joint. Make sure that the whole surface of the joint is covered with a thin film of glue, then apply pressure by clamping for an hour. If you do not have G-cramps or a suitable vice, then the two pieces can be bound together with taut masking tape until the join has bonded. PVA is water resistant but not weatherproof, so it should only be used for interior work if the finished work is not sealed.

SAWING

You should always saw a piece of wood on the waste side of your cutting line. A handsaw should be used to saw your lengths of timber to size before any fine work begins. Mark out a cutting line with a soft pencil against a try square, then score along the marked line with a craft knife – this will give the top edge of the wood a smooth finish. Use G-cramps or a vice to secure the wood when making the first few cuts (the idea is to make a channel for the saw blade to follow). Then remove the cramps and, holding the wood near to the blade with your spare hand, gently saw into the wood, keeping the blade lowered and supporting the wood from below for the last strokes. Always ensure that your saw is sharp.

MEASURING WINDOWS

Before starting to make curtains, you must first measure the window to calculate how much fabric is needed. This is a very important calculation, so take your time and check your measurements again once you have finished.

If possible, fix the track, pole or pelmet board in place before measuring the window. The track or pole should be attached 5–15 cm (2–6 in) above the window frame, with the ends projecting at least 10 cm (4 in) beyond each side of the window. Take measurements with a metal tape measure, and if the window is very tall or wide get someone to help you.

The two measurements needed to calculate fabric quantities for a pair of curtains are the width and the length of the window. To work out the width of the finished curtains, measure the width of the track, rail or pole. If you are using a pelmet board, measure the sides and front. To calculate the drop of the finished full-length curtains, measure from the top of the track or bottom of the pole to the floor. For sill-length curtains, measure from the top of the track or bottom of the pole to the sill. For apron-length curtains, measure from the top of the track or pole to just below the sill or to the desired point.

BASTING STITCH

This temporary stitch is like a larger, looser version of running stitch. It holds fabric in place until it is permanently stitched. Use a colourful thread so the basting is clearly visible and therefore easy to remove.

SLIP STITCH

Slip stitch holds a folded edge to flat fabric or two folded edges together, as in a mitred corner. Work on the wrong side of the fabric, from right to left. Start with the needle in the fold. Push it out and pick up a few threads from the flat fabric, then insert it into the hem again, all in one smooth and continuous movement. When finished, the stitches should be almost invisible.

BLANKET STITCH

A decorative stitch for finishing edges. Secure the thread at one end of the fabric, and working from right to left, insert the needle about 1 cm (½ in) from the edge; keep the thread under the point of the needle and complete the stitch to create a loop. Continue to work the stitches every 1 cm (½ in) or so, making sure the height is even.

MITRING CORNERS

Mitring is the neatest and tidiest way of working hem corners. Press in the hem allowance along the bottom and sides of the fabric, then open it out flat again. Where the two fold lines meet, turn in the corner of the fabric diagonally. Turn in the hems along the pressed fold to form a neat diagonal line. Use slip stitch to secure.

MAKING TIES AND TABS

To make a tie, cut a strip of material to the desired width and length. Fold the strip in half along the length, wrong sides together, and press. Pin, baste and machine-sew all along the long side and one short end, leaving the other short end unstitched. Push the tie right side out with the aid of a knitting needle. Turn in a 5 mm (¼ in) fold to the inside of the tie, press in place and slip-stitch the end closed. Tabs are made in exactly the same way as ties – the only difference is that the strip of fabric is wider and they are usually buttoned, not tied.

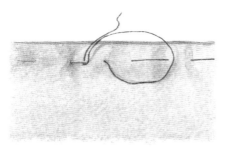

Basting stitch

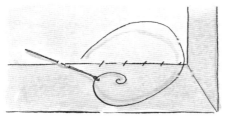

Slip stitch

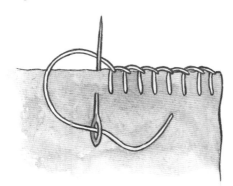

Blanket stitch

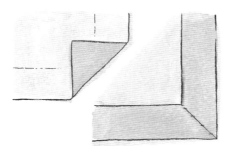

Mitring corners

Making ties and tabs

sources

Baileys Home & Garden
The Engine Shed
Station Approach
Ross-on-Wye
Herefordshire HR9 7BW
t. 01989 561931
www.baileyshomeandgarden.co.uk
Vintage, retro, recycled and new things – from baths to bird feeders – for the home, garden, children and pets.

Belle Maison
t. 01403 822440 for stockists
www.bellemaison.com
Hand-painted furniture in styles including Provençal and Swedish.

Bennison
16 Holbein Place
London SW1W 8NL
t. 020 7730 8076
www.bennisonfabrics.com
Hand-printed fabrics based on 18th- and 19th- century English and French textiles.

Bergeres and Chairs
Round Street
Cobham
Kent DA13 9AY
t. 01474 813445
www.bergeresandchairs.co.uk
Antique bergere sofas, chairs and suites, from the UK and Europe, restored and upholstered in modern designer fabric.

Bespoke Country Collection
18 Bar Street
Scarborough
North Yorkshire YO11 2HT
t. 01723 378728
www.bespokecountrycollection.com
Vintage country, Shaker-style and folk-art interior accessories; also paints and fabrics.

Bessie and George
3 St Peter's Hill, Flushing,
Falmouth, Cornwall TR11 5TP
t. 01326 373089
www.bessieandgeorge.com
Hand-made items that bring the coast to your home, including cushions, bunting, laundry bags and dog beds.

The Blue Door
74 Church Road
London SW13 0DQ
t. 020 8748 9785
www.thebluedoor.co.uk
Reproduction Gustavian painted furniture, plus fabrics, lighting and accessories.

Capella
Unit 2, Central Court
Finch Close
Nottingham NG7 2NN
t. 0845 148 0015
www.capellaretail.com
Printed English textiles including bedlinen, table linen, cushions, notebooks and photograph albums.

Caroline Zoob
Shop A, 33 Cliffe High Street
Lewes
East Sussex BN7 2AN
t. 01273 476464
www.carolinezoob.com
Hand-made and antique collectables, including cushions and pictures made from antique textiles, painted china, vintage blankets, patchwork quilts and decorative antiques.

Cast in Style
3 Coalway Road, Penn
Wolverhampton WV3 7LR
t. 01902 765000/334776 (shop)
Makers of cast-iron products (in their own foundry), including hanging racks, knobs, knockers, locks, pulls and boot scrapers.

Cath Kidston
t. 020 7935 6555
www.cathkidston.co.uk
Distinctive printed fabrics, oilcloths and textile accessories; also china, glassware, cutlery, enamelware.

Chandlers
Freepost Chandlers
t. 0870 2401123
Hand-crafted and traditional home accessories and gifts by post, including enamelware, blue-and-white china, baskets and clocks.

Classic Quilts
The Old Bakery
Charlton Marshall
Blandford Forum
Dorset DT11 9NH
t. 01258 453913
Hand-crafted quilts in a variety of patterns and sizes.

Country Home & Garden Antiques
The Parkhouse Antique Centre
Hewetts Kiln
Tongham Road
Rufold, Farnham
Surrey GU10 1PQ
t. 07778 022692
www.online-ceramics.com
Antique distressed furniture, enamelware, kitchenalia and vintage chintz reproduction jugs.

Decorative Living
55 New Kings Road
London SW6 4SE
t. 020 7736 5623
www.decorativeliving.co.uk
Unusual antique and new furniture; also upholstery, restoration, rewiring and paint effects.

Designgate
Old Parish Poorhouse
Bank Top, Winster
Derbyshire DE4 2DR
t. 01629 650508
www.designgate.co.uk
Unique interior accessories including clocks, mirrors, blackboards, furniture and lights, all hand-made from reclaimed materials.

Ella's Kitchen Company
The Dower House, Cheney
Longville
Craven Arms SY7 8DR
t. 01588 673976
www.ellaskitchencompany.com
Norwegian kitchen cabinets and traditional kitchen utensils.

Fair and Weathered
7 Union Street, Harleston
Norfolk IP20 9BO
t. 07979 593096
www.fairandweathered.com
Shabby chateau chic home and garden furniture and accessories, sourced from around Europe.

Farrow & Ball
Uddens Estate, Wimborne
Dorset BH21 7NL
t. 01202 876141
www.farrow-ball.co.uk
Paint and wallpaper made using traditional methods.

Forever England
6 The Old Yarn Business Centre
Westbury, Sherborne
Dorset DT9 3RQ
t. 01935 811970
0870 241 6517 (mail order)
www.foreverengland.net
Quilts, bedding and lighting, and antique French beds.

French Collectables
Church View House
26 High Street
Bushey WD23 3HL
t. 020 8950 0930
www.frenchcollectables.com
Unusual, characterful and sometimes rare French antiques for the home.

The French House
PO Box 400
Southampton SO14 0TH
t. 0870 9014547
Traditional French products made by artisans and small family firms.

Gooseberry Tart
Pigeons Piece, Horseshoe Lane,
Wootton by Woodstock
Oxon OX20 1DR
t. 01993 810681
www.gooseberrytart.com
*Antique and collectable
kitchenalia, plus knitted tea cosies,
kitchen fairies and aprons, and
cushions made from vintage and
reproduction fabric.*

Grand Illusions
PO Box 81, Shaftesbury
Dorset SP7 8TA
t. 01747 858300
www.grandillusions.co.uk
*Unique country-style accessories
for the home and garden.*

Ian Mankin
109 Regent's Park Road
London NW1 8UR
t. 020 7722 0997
Natural and utility fabrics.

Imogen Jamieson
t. 020 8942 2108
www.imogenjamieson.co.uk
*Constantly changing stock of old
French and English furniture,
garden tables and accessories,
decorative items and kitchenalia.*

Inside Outdoors
The North Lodge
London Minstead
Hampshire SO43 7FT
t. 07909 522727
www.insideoutdoors.com
*Unique and individual furnishings
and accessories for the home and
garden.*

Kate Forman Fabrics
The Annexe
Byways
Ashford Lane
Steep
Petersfield
Hampshire GU32 1AD
t. 01730 233592
www.kateforman.co.uk
*French vintage- and country-
influenced fabrics, sold by the
metre and made up into
household accessories such as
cushions, place mats and lampshades.*

**La Maison de Provence/
Just Sew**
Alfold House
Alfold
Surrey GU6 8HP
t. 01403 753968
*French country and Provençal
table linen, kitchen and garden
accessories, fabric bags, baskets
and gifts.*

Labour and Wait
18 Cheshire Street
London E2 6EH
t. 020 7729 6253
www.labourandwait.co.uk
*Timeless, functional products for
daily life.*

Living Vintage
113d Northcote Road
London SW11 6PN
t. 020 7223 4440
*Antique quilts and eiderdowns,
cushions, pictures and scented
gifts.*

Louise Loves
19 Stanley Street
Southport
Merseyside PR9 0BY
t. 01704 538606
www.louiseloves.co.uk
*Vintage and vintage-inspired
fabrics, lighting, quilts, blankets
and kitchenalia.*

Melin Tregwynt
Castle Morris
Haverford West
Pembrokeshire SA62 5UX
t. 01348 891225
*Classic and contemporary
blankets, cushions, throws and
accessories.*

Mole and Cheese
20 Cowper Road
Berkhamsted
Hertfordshire HP4 3DE
t. 01442 871408
*www.moleandcheese.co.uk
A range of retro-inspired home
accessories.*

The Old Potting Shed
t. 0118 933 1510
www.thevintagelook.co.uk
*Vintage-style home accessories,
including enamelware and wirework.*

Re
Bishops Yard
Main Street
Corbridge
Northumberland NE45 5LA
t. 01434 634567
www.re-foundobjects.com
*Recycled, restored and remarkable
objects from around the world.*

Really Rural
The Sanctuary
Okehampton
Devon EX20 4AL
t. 01822 820203
www.reallyrural.co.uk
*Hand-painted furniture and
accessories designed to capture
the charm of rural England.*

RK Alliston
173 New Kings Road
London SW6 4SW
t. 0845 130 5577
www.rkalliston.com
*Decorative and practical things for
the garden and home.*

Roger Oates
t. 01531 631611
for showrooms and stockists
www.rogeroates.com
Stair runners, rugs and fabrics.

Room Remedies
12 Lambton Road
Raynes Park
London SW20 1CR
t. 020 8946 6894
www.roomremedies.co.uk
Reproduction period-style lighting.

Salvo
www.salvo.co.uk
*Architectural salvage, garden
antiques, reclaimed building
materials and reproduction.*

Shaker
21 Market Place
Tetbury
Gloucestershire GL8 8DD
t. 0845 331 2055
www.shaker.co.uk
*Traditional Shaker furniture and
accessories.*

Simply Living
22 North Hill
Colchester
Essex CO1 1EG
t. 01206 367333
www.simply-living.co.uk
*Furnishings, accessories and an
interior design service with an aim
of creating pure and seamless
living spaces.*

The Somerset Gallery
Woodcock Farmhouse
Rodden, Frome
Somerset BA11 5LD
t. 01373 832460
www.the-somerset-gallery.com
*Hand-made interior accessories,
including Shaker-style peg rails,
knitted cushions, clocks, mirrors
and tea cosies.*

Steve Handley
24 Rushworth Avenue
West Bridgeford
Nottingham NG2 7LF
t. 0115 982 0427
www.stevehandley.co.uk
*Cupboards, dressers, chairs,
tables, beds and hooks made
from reclaimed timber and found
objects.*

Susie Watson Designs
River House Studio
Axford
Nr Marlborough
Wiltshire SN8 2HA
t. 01672 520604
*Hand-made kitchen china in
delightful shapes and colours.*

Swedish Chic
45 East Road
London E15 3QS
t. 020 8472 7700
www.swedish-chic.com
*Swedish chandeliers, ceramics,
baskets and enamelware.*

Vanessa Arbuthnott Fabrics
t. 01285 831437
www.vanessaarbuthnott.co.uk
*Traditional fabrics inspired by life
in rural England, seaside holidays
and Italian landscapes. Also
wallpaper and pottery.*

picture credits

Key: *ph= photographer, il= illustrator, a=above, b=below, r=right, l=left, c=centre.*

Endpapers ph Christopher Drake; **1** ph Christopher Drake/refurbishment and interior design by Chichi Meroni Fassio, Parnassus; **2** Polly Eltes/Sheila Scholes' house near Cambridge; **3** ph James Merrell/Hotel de la Mirande; **4al & br** ph Simon Upton; **4c** ph Caroline Arber; **5** ph Catherine Gratwicke/designer Caroline Zoob's home in East Sussex; **7** ph Simon Upton; **9** ph James Merrell; **10al** ph Alan Williams/the Norfolk home of Geoff and Gilly Newberry of Bennison Fabrics– on walls: Tulip Tree in pink and green on beige linen by Bennison; **10–11a** ph Alan Williams/Louise Robbins' house in North West Herefordshire; **10bl** ph Jan Baldwin/Mark Smith's home in the Cotswolds; **10br** ph Chris Everard/a house in London designed by Helen Ellery of The Plot London, paintings by Robert Clarke; **11ar** ph Alan Williams/the Norfolk home of Geoff and Gilly Newberry of Bennison Fabrics-on walls: Daisy Chain on oyster linen; **11bl** ph Tom Leighton/Marilyn Phipps' house in Kent; **12al** ph Simon Upton; **12ac** ph James Merrell/Mary Drysdale; **12–13a** ph Simon Upton/the home of Julia and Glen Vague, Kentucky, designed by Jacomini Interior Design; **12–13b** ph Simon Upton/the Jacomini Family Farm, designed by Jacomini Interior Design; **13a** ph Simon Upton/Mrs Robin Elverson's house near Round Top, Texas; **13b** ph James Merrell; **14a** ph Christopher Drake/Alain and Catherine Brunel's home and hotel, La Maison Douce, Saint-Martin de Ré; **14bl** ph Tom Leighton; **14br** ph Simon Upton; **15a** both ph Christopher Drake/Florence and Pierre Pallardy, Domaine de la Baronnie, St-Martin de Ré; **16al & ac** ph Polly Wreford/Lena Proudlock's home Gloucestershire has since been restyled; **16–17a & 16–17b** ph Simon Upton/Lena Proudlock's home Gloucestershire has since been restyled; **17ac** ph Christopher Drake/Nordic Style Bedroom; **17ar** ph Simon Upton/Lena Proudlock's home Gloucestershire has since been restyled; **17br** ph James Merrell; **19** ph David Montgomery/Sheila Scholes' house near Cambridge; **20al** ph Christopher Drake/Julie Prisca's home in Normandy; **20bl** ph James Merrell; **20ac & 20–21a** Simon Upton/the home of Julia and Glen Vague, Kentucky, designed by Jacomini Interior Design; **20c & 20–21b** Simon Upton; **22al & bl** ph Christopher Drake/owners of La Cour Beaudeval Antiquities, Mireille and Jean Claude Lothon's house in Faverolles; **22ar** ph Polly Wreford/Mary Foley's house in Connecticut; **23a** ph Alan Williams/the Norfolk home of Geoff and Gilly Newberry of Bennison Fabrics- on walls: Chinese pheasant on oatmeal linen by Bennison; **23b** ph Christopher Drake/Lee Freund's Summerhouse in Southampton, New York; **24l** ph Alan Williams/the Arbuthnott family's house near Cirencester designed by Nicholas Arbuthnott, fabrics designed by Vanessa Arbuthnott; **24c** ph Tom Leighton; **24–25** ph Alan Williams/Miv Watts' house in Norfolk; **26** ph David Montgomery, **26–27** il Michael Hill; **28al** ph Polly Wreford/The Sawmills Studios; **28bl** ph Christopher Drake/Florence and Pierre Pallardy, Domaine de la Baronnie, St-Martin de Ré; **28ac** ph James Merrell/cushions from The Blue Door; **28ar** ph Christopher Drake/owner Monique Davidson's family home in Normandy; **28cr** ph Catherine Gratwicke/interior designer Sue West's house in Gloucestershire-selection of cushions on sofa made by Sue West; **28br** ph David Montgomery/Sasha Waddell's house in London; **29l** ph James Merrell; **29r** ph Debi Treloar/Mark and Sally of Baileys Home & Garden's house in Herefordshire; **30a** ph Catherine Gratwicke/interior designer Sue West's house in Gloucestershire – blind made from tea-towel-style fabric from The Housemade; **30b** ph Catherine Gratwicke/designer Caroline Zoob's home in East Sussex – selection of cushions made from antique fabric by Caroline Zoob, blind made from antique linen; **30–31** ph Polly Eltes/blind design by Sian and Annie Colley; **32** ph James Merrell/fabrics from Sandersons, ties from John Lewis; **32–33** il Jacqueline Pestell; **34al** ph Jan Baldwin/the owner of Tessuti, Catherine Vindevogel-Debal's house in Kortrijk, Belgium; **34bl** ph Caroline Arber/Linda Garman's home in London; **34bc** ph Henry Bourne; **34br** ph Caroline Arber; **35** ph Caroline Arber/Linda Garman's home in London; **36l** ph James Merrell; **36r** ph Chris Everard/a house in London designed by Helen Ellery of The Plot London; **37a** ph Christopher Drake/Josephine Ryan's house in London; **37bl & br** ph James Merrell; **37bc** ph David Montgomery; **38** ph James Merrell; **38–39** il Lizzie Sanders; **40** ph James Merrell; **40–41** il Helen Smythe; **42al** ph David Montgomery/a house in Connecticut designed by Lynn Morgan Design; **42bl** ph David

Montgomery/Sasha Waddell's house in London; **42–43a** ph Simon Upton; **42br** ph Henry Bourne; **43b** ph James Merrell; **44al** ph Simon Upton; **44–45** ph James Merrell; **45ar** ph Simon Upton/Lena Proudlock's home Gloucestershire has since been restyled; **45br** ph Christopher Drake/owners of La Cour Beaudeval Antiquities, Mireille and Jean Claude Lothon's house in Faverolles; **46al** ph James Merrell; **46ar & 47** ph James Merrell/Mary Drysdale; **48al** ph Catherine Gratwicke/owner of Adamczewski, Hélène Adamczewski's house in Lewes – antique patchwork quilt from Grace & Favour; **48cl & bl** ph David Montgomery/Sasha Waddell's house in London; **48–49a** ph Henry Bourne; **48–49b** ph Christopher Drake/owners of La Cour Beaudeval Antiquities, Mireille and Jean Claude Lothon's house in Faverolles; **49** ph David Montgomery; **50al** ph David Montgomery/a house in Connecticut designed by Lynn Morgan Design; **50ar** ph Christopher Drake/Nordic Style; **50br** ph Simon Upton/a residence in Highlands, North Carolina, designed by Nancy Braithwaite Interiors; **51al** ph Henry Bourne; **51ar** ph Simon Upton; **51b** ph James Merrell; **52** ph Christopher Drake/Mr and Mrs Degrugillier, Le Mas de Flore, Antiquite et Creation, Lagnes, Isle sur Sorgue, Provence; patchwork tablecloth, tea service and plates, L'Utile e il Dilettevole; **52–53** il Lizzie Sanders; **54al** ph Christopher Drake/Lincoln Cato's house in Brighton; **54ar** ph Henry Bourne; **54b** both Polly Wreford; **55b** Catherine Gratwicke/the home of Patty Collister in London, owner of An Angel At My Table-jug cover from the Dining Room Shop, place mats from Tobias & The Angel; **55a** ph Caroline Arber/Linda Garman's home in London; **56** ph James Merrell; **56–57** il Lizzie Sanders; **58al** ph Andrew Wood; **58bl** ph James Merrell/Baron and Baroness de Mitri de Gunzburg's house in Provence; **58–59a** ph James Merrell/Janick and Hubert Schoumacher-Vilfroy's house in Normandy; **59c** ph Christopher Drake/interior designer Carole Oulhen; **59b** ph David Montgomery/Sheila Scholes' house near Cambridge; **60al** ph James Merrell/Mr and Mrs Barrow's house in Surrey designed by architects Marshall Haines and Barrow/kitchen by Chalon; **60–61a** ph James Merrell/Vicky and Simon Young's house in Northumberland; **61b** ph Simon Upton/Conner Prairie open-air living museum; **61a** ph Alan Williams/Louise Robbins' house in northwest Herefordshire; **62al** ph Tom Leighton/paint Farrow & Ball: floor Mouse's Back floor paint no. 40, cupboards Green Smoke no. 47 and interior Red Fox no. 48, walls and woodwork String no. 8, ceiling Off White no. 3; **62ar** ph James Merrell; **62b** ph Polly Wreford; **63a** ph Christopher Drake/Florence and Pierre Pallardy, Domaine de la Baronnie, St-Martin de Ré; **63b** ph Andrew Wood; **64** ph David Montgomery; **64–65** il Michael Hill; **66al** ph James Merrell; **66bl** ph Simon Upton; **66ar** ph Caroline Arber; **66cr & 67a** ph Catherine Gratwicke/designer Caroline Zoob's home in East Sussex – patchwork curtains made by Caroline Zoob from antique fabric; **66br & 67bl** ph Catherine Gratwicke/owner of Adamczewski, Hélène Adamczewski's house in Lewes – antique ticking on table and in cupboard from Kim Sully Antiques, all ceramics from Adamczewski; **67br** ph Christopher Drake/Ali Sharland's former home in Gloucestershire; **68l** ph James Merrell; **68r** ph Simon Upton/Plain English; **69a & 69bl** ph Catherine Gratwicke/interior designer Sue West's house in Gloucestershire – linen covered notebooks and napkin box with initial from The Housemade; **69bc** ph Polly Wreford/Linda Garman's home in London, patchwork tablecloth by Rob Merrett; **69br** ph Catherine Gratwicke/Claudia Bryant's house in London – glove from Grace & Favour, lined with Liberty print fabric; **70** ph James Merrell; **70–71** il Michael Hill; **72a** ph Simon Upton/Plain English; **72bl** ph Tom Leighton; **72br** ph Henry Bourne; **73al** ph Christopher Drake/Annie-Camille Kuentzmann-Levet's house in the Yvelines; **73ar** ph Christopher Drake/owner Monique Davidson's family home in Normandy; **73b** ph Simon Upton; **74** ph Christopher Drake/Lincoln Cato's house in Brighton; **75a & bl** ph Simon Upton/Plain English; **75bc** ph Simon Upton; **75br** ph Caroline Arber; **76** ph David Montgomery; **76–77** il Michael Hill; **78al** ph James Merrell/Hotel Villa Gallici; **78ac & c** ph Christopher Drake/Ali Sharland's former home in Gloucestershire; **78bl** ph Jan Baldwin/Michael D'Souza of Mufti; **78–79a** ph Tom Leighton/Fay and Roger Oates' house in Ledbury; **78–79b** ph Jan Baldwin/a house in Maine designed by Stephen Blatt Architects; **80a** ph Tom Leighton; **80b** ph Christopher Drake/Warner Johnson's apartment in New York designed by Edward Cabot of Cabot Design Ltd.; **80–81** ph Tom Leighton; **81a** ph Alan Williams/the Arbuthnott family's house near Cirencester designed by Nicholas Arbuthnott, fabrics designed by Vanessa Arbuthnott; **81b** ph Alan Williams/Louise Robbins' house in northwest Herefordshire; **82al** ph Chris Everard/a house in London designed by Helen Ellery of The Plot London, paintings by Robert Clarke; **82bl** ph Tom Leighton; **82ar** ph Ray Main/Marina and Peter Hill's barn in West Sussex designed by Marina Hill, Peter James Construction Management, Chichester, The West

Sussex Antique Timber Company, Wisborough Green, and Joanna Jefferson Architects; **83al** ph Christopher Drake/Alain and Catherine Brunel's home and hotel, La Maison Douce, Saint-Martin de Ré; **83ar** ph James Merrell; **83b** ph James Merrell/architect, Jim Ruscitto; **84** ph James Merrell; **84–85** il Helen Smythe; **86a** ph Catherine Gratwicke/designer Caroline Zoob's home in East Sussex – lampshade an original design by Caroline Zoob; **86c** ph Henry Bourne; **86b** Nelly Guyot's house in Ramatuelle, France, styled by Nelly Guyot; **87l** ph David Montgomery/Sasha Waddell's house in London; **87c** ph Catherine Gratwicke/Rose Hammick's home in London – covered box from Braemar Antiques, button bag from An Angel At My Table; **87b** ph Christopher Drake/owners of French Country Living, the Hill family's home on the Côte d'Azur; **87ar** ph Debi Treloar; **88a** ph James Merrell; **88bl** ph Catherine Gratwicke; **88bc** ph Christopher Drake/owners of La Cour Beaudeval Antiquities, Mireille and Jean Claude Lothon's house in Faverolles; **88br** ph Catherine Gratwicke; **89al** ph Christopher Drake/owner Monique Davidson's family home in Normandy; **89ar** ph Christopher Drake/Annie-Camille Kuentzmann-Levet's house in the Yvelines; **90** ph Catherine Gratwicke/Rose Hammick's home in London, quilt made by Lucinda Ganderton; **90–91** il Lizzie Sanders; **92al, ar & br** ph James Merrell; **92cr** ph Christopher Drake/Tita Bay's village house in Ramatuelle; **92bl** ph Caroline Arber; **93a** ph Christopher Drake/Alain and Catherine Brunel's home and hotel, La Maison Douce, Saint-Martin de Ré; **93b** ph Jan Baldwin/Roderick and Gillie James' house in Devon designed by Roderick James Architects and built by Carpenter Oak & Woodland Co. Ltd; **94** ph Sandra Lane; **94–95** il Lizzie Sanders; **96al** ph Chris Everard/Emma & Neil's house in London, walls painted by Garth Carter; **96bl** ph Christopher Drake/Eva Johnson's house in Suffolk, interiors designed by Eva Johnson; **96–97a** ph Christopher Drake/interior designer Carole Oulhen; **96–97b** ph Christopher Drake/Enrica Stabile's house in Le Thor, Provence; **97b** ph Simon Upton/a residence in Highlands, North Carolina, designed by Nancy Braithwaite Interiors; **98al** ph Christopher Drake/owner Monique Davidson's family home in Normandy; **98ar** ph Jan Baldwin/a house in Maine designed by Stephen Blatt Architects; **98b** ph Simon Upton/a residence in Highlands, North Carolina, designed by Nancy Braithwaite Interiors; **99al** ph Ray Main/Marina and Peter Hill's barn in West Sussex designed by Marina Hill, Peter James Construction Management, Chichester, The West Sussex Antique Timber Company, Wisborough Green, and Joanna Jefferson Architects; **99ar** ph James Merrell; **99b** ph Christopher Drake/Eva Johnson's house in Suffolk, interiors designed by Eva Johnson; **100a** ph Catherine Gratwicke/designer Caroline Zoob's home in East Sussex – floral Dorothy bag made by Caroline Zoob; **100bl** ph Henry Bourne/Fay and Roger Oates' house in Ledbury; **100bc** ph James Merrell; **100br** Simon Upton/a residence in Highlands, North Carolina, designed by Nancy Braithwaite Interiors; **101** ph James Merrell; **102l** ph Christopher Drake/Enrica Stabile's house in Brunello; **102c** ph James Merrell; **102r** ph Catherine Gratwicke/interior designer Sue West's house in Gloucestershire – pink mug and toile-edged towels from Grace & Favour; **103** ph James Merrell; **104, 105ac & 105bc** il Michael Hill; **105a & b** il Lizzie Sanders; **105c** il Jacqueline Pestell.

Architects and designers whose work is featured in this book

Adamczewski
fine houseware
88 High Street
Lewes
East Sussex, BN7 1XN
t. 01273 470105
adamczewski@onetel.net.uk
pages 48al, 66br, 67bl

An Angel At My Table
t. 020 7424 9777
www.angelatmytable.co.uk
pages 55b, 87c

Annie-Camille Kuentzmann-Levet
Décoration
3 Ter, Rue Mathieu Le Coz
La Noue
78980 Mondreville
France
t./f. +33 1 30 42 53 59
pages 73al, 89ar

Arne Maynard Garden Design
71 New Kings Road
London, SW6 4SQ
pages 24c, 80–81a

Baileys Home & Garden
The Engine Shed
Station Approach
Ross-on-Wye
Herefordshire, HR9 7BW
t. 01989 563015
f. 01989 768172
sales@baileys-home-garden.co.uk
www.baileyshomeandgarden.com
page 29r

Bennison Fabrics
16 Holbein Place
London, SW1W 8NL
t. 020 7730 8076
f. 020 7823 4997
bennisonfabrics@btinternet.com
www.bennisonfabrics.com
pages 10al, 11ar, 23a

Cabot Design Ltd.
interior design
1925 Seventh Avenue, Suite 71
New York, NY 10026
USA
t. +1 212 222 9488
eocabot@aol.com
page 80b

Carole Oulhen
interior designer
t. +33 6 80 99 66 16
f. +33 4 90 02 01 91
pages 59c, 96–97a

Caroline Zoob
Shop A
33 Cliffe High Street
Lewes
East Sussex, BN7 2AN
t. 01273 476464
(shop & mail order)
www.carolinezoob.com
hand-made collectables
pages 5, 30b, 66cr, 67a, 86a, 100a

Carpenter Oak Ltd.
The Framing Yard
East Cornworthy
Totnes
Devon, TQ9 7HF
t. 01803 732900
www.carpenteroak.com
page 93b

Conner Prairie
open-air living history museum
13400 Allisonville Road
Fishers, IN 46038
USA
t. +1 800 966 1836
www.connerprairie.org
page 61b

Claudia Bryant
t. 020 7602 2852
page 69br

Domaine de la Baronnie
21 Rue Baron de Chantal
17410 Saint-Martin-de-Ré
France
t. +33 5 46 09 21 29
f. +33 5 46 09 95 29
info@domainedelabaronnie.com
www.domainedelabaronnie.com
pages 15a both, 28bl, 63a

Enrica Stabile
antiques dealer, interior decorator
and photographic stylist
L'Utile e il Dilettevole
Via Carlo Maria Maggi 6
20154 Milano
Italy
t. +39 0234 53 60 86
www.enricastabile.com
pages 52–53, 96–97b, 102l

Eva Johnson
interior designer
t 01638 731 362
f 01638 731 855
www.evajohnson.com
distributor of TRIP TRAP wood
floor treatment products
pages 96bl, 99b

Farrow & Ball
Uddens Estate
Wimborne
Dorset, BH21 7NL
t. 01202 876141
f. 01202 873793
www.farrowandball.com
page 62al

French Country Living
antiques and decoration
21 Rue De L'Eglise
06250 Mougins
France
t. +33 4 93 75 53 03
f. +33 4 93 75 63 03
f.c.l.com@wanadoo.fr
page 87b

Garth Carter
t 07958 412953
page 96al

Helen Ellery
The Plot London
interior design
77 Compton Street
London, EC1V 0BN
t. 020 7251 8116
f. 020 7251 8117
helen@theplotlondon.com
www.theplotlondon.com
pages 10br, 36r, 82al

Hotel de la Mirande
Avignon
France
page 3

Hotel Villa Gallici
Aix-en-Provence
France
page 78al

J&M Davidson
Gallery;
97 Golborne Road
London W10 5NL
Shop;
42 Ledbury Road
London W11 2SE
pages 28ar, 73ar, 89al, 98al

Jacomini Interior Design
1701 Brun Street, Suite 101
Houston TX 77019
USA
t. +1 713 524 8224
f. +1 713 524 0951
www.jacominidesign.com
pages 12–13a, 12–13b, 20ac, 20–21a

Jim Ruscitto, Architect
Ruscitto, Latham, Blanton
PO Box 419
Sun Valley Idaho
ID 83353
USA
f. +1 208 726 1033
page 83b

Joanna Jefferson Architects
222 Oving Road
Chichester
West Sussex PO19 4EJ
t. 01243 532398
f. 01243 531550
jjeffearch@aol.com
pages 82ar, 99al

Josephine Ryan
antiques and interiors
63 Abbeville Road
London SW4 9JW
t. 020 8675 3900
page 37a

Julie Prisca
46 Rue du Bac
75007 Paris
France
t. +33 1 45 48 13 29
infos@julieprisca.com
www.julieprisca.com
page 20al

La Maison Douce
25 rue Mérindot
17410 St-Martin-de-Ré
France
t. +33 546 09 20 20
t. +33 546 09 09 90
www.lamaisondouce.com
pages 14a, 83al, 93a

Lena Proudlock
www.lenaproudlock.com
pages 16, 16–17a, 16–17b, 17ar, 45ar

Lincoln Cato
t. 01273 325334
pages 54al, 74

Louise Robbins
Insideout House and Garden
Agency and Malt House
Bed & Breakfast
Malt House, Almeley,
Herefordshire, HR3 6PY
t. 01544 340681
lulawrence1@aol.com
www.insideout
-house&garden.co.uk
pages 10–11a, 61a, 81b

Lynn Morgan Design
118 Goodwives River Road
Darien, CT 06820
USA
pages 42al, 50l

Mark Smith at Smithcreative
15 St Georges Road
London, W4 1AU
t. 020 8747 3909
f. 020 8742 3902
mark@smithcreative.net
ceramics by David Garland
t. 01285 720307
page 10bl

Marshall Haines and Barrow
Gresham House
24 Holburn Viaduct
London EC1A 2BN
t. 020 7248 6622
www.mhbdesigngroup.com
page 60al

Mary Drysdale
Drysdale, Inc
78 Kalorama Cir NW
Washington DC 20008
USA
t. +1 202 588 0700
pages 12ac, 46ar, 47

Mireille and Jean Claude Lothon
La Cour Beaudeval Antiquities
4 rue des Fontaines
28210 Faverolles
France
t. +33 2 37 51 47 67
pages 22al, 22bl, 45br, 48–49b, 88bc

Miv Watts Design
House Bait I
t. 01328 730557
House Bait II
t. 01328 730583
www.wattswishedfor.com
pages 24–25

Mufti
789 Fulham Road
London SW6 5HA
t. 020 7610 9123
f. 020 7384 2050
www.mufti.co.uk
pages 78bl

Nancy Braithwaite Interiors
2300 Peachtree Road
Suite C101
Atlanta, GA 30309
USA
t. +1 404 355 1740
f. +1 404 355 8693
pages 50br, 97b, 98b, 101br

Nelly Guyot
Décoratrice
t. +33 6 09 25 20 68
page 86b

Nordic Style
Classic Swedish Interiors
109 Lots Road
London SW10 0RN
t. 020 7351 1755
www.nordicstyle.com
pages 17ac, 50ar

Parnassus
corso Porta Vittoria, 5
Milan
Italy
t. +39 02 78 11 07
page 1

Peter Hone
garden antique consultant,
appointments only
5 Ladbroke Square
London W11 3LX
page 82bl

Plain English
cupboardmakers
Stowupland Hall
Stowupland
Stowmarket
Suffolk IP14 4BE
t. 01449 774028
www.plainenglishdesign.com
page 68r, 72a, 75a, 75bl

Roderick James Architects
Seagull House
Dittisham Mill Creek
Dartmouth
Devon TQ6 0HZ
t. 01803 722474
www.roderickjamesarchitects.com
page 93b

Roger Oates
London Showroom
1 Munro Terrace (off Riley Street)
London SW10 0DL
t. 020 7351 2288
Eastnor Shop
The Long Barn, Eastnor
Herefordshire HR8 1EL
t. 01531 631611
www.rogeroates.co.uk
pages 78–79a, 100bl

Sasha Waddell
269 Wandsworth Bridge Road
London SW6 2TX
t. 020 7736 0766
pages 28br, 42bl, 48cl, 48bl, 87l

Sharland & Lewis
52 Long Street
Tetbury
Gloucester GL8 8AQ
t. 01666 500354
www.sharlandandlewis.com
pages 67br, 78ac, 78c

Sheila Scholes
designer
t. 01480 498241
pages 2, 19, 59b

Sian Colley Soft Furnishings
Block E 2B Upper Ringway
Bounds Green
London N11 2UD
t./f. 020 8368 4092
colleysian@hotmail.com
pages 30–31

Stephen Blatt Architects
10 Danforth Street
Portland
Maine 04112–0583
USA
t. +1 207 761 5911
www.sbarchitects.com
pages 78–79b, 98ar

Story
4 Wilkes Street
London E1 6QF
t. 020 7377 0313
page 62b

Sue West
The Housemade
interior & product design
t./f. 01453 757771
sue.west@btopenworld.com
www.avaweb.co.uk/coachhouse
.html
pages 28cr, 30a, 69a, 69bl, 102r

Tessuti
interiors & fabrics
Doorniksewijk 76
8500 Kortrijk
Belgium
t. +32 56 25 29 27
info@tessuti.be
www.tessuti.be
page 34al

Tita Bay
interior decorator
via Sudorno, 22D
24100 Bergamo
Italy
t. +39 03 52 58 384
page 92cr

Vanessa Arbuthnott fabrics:
www.vanessaarbuthnott.co.uk
holiday lets: www.thetallet.co.uk
pages 24l, 81a

index

Copyright information (continued from page 4)
All projects have been previously published by Ryland, Peters & Small

page 26 Display frame
Project taken from *Painted Woodcraft* by Sally and Stewart Walton, © 1997

page 32 Linen cushion cover
Project taken from *Katrin Cargill's Simple Cushions* by Katrin Cargill, © 1996

page 38 Pumpkin display
Project taken from *Paula Pryke's Candles* by Paula Pryke, © 1998

page 40 Autumn wreath
Project taken from *Paula Pryke's Candles* by Paula Pryke, © 1998

page 52 Floral tablecloth
Project taken from *Open Air Living* by Enrica Stabile, © 2001

page 56 Hop centrepiece
Project taken from *Paula Pryke's Candles* by Paula Pryke, © 1998

page 64 Plate rack
Project taken from *Painted Woodcraft* by Sally and Stewart Walton, © 1997

page 70 Yellow-checked curtains
Project taken from *Katrin Cargill's Simple Curtains* by Katrin Cargill, © 1996

page 76 Key cupboard
Project taken from *Painted Woodcraft* by Sally and Stewart Walton, © 1997

page 84 Driftwood frame
Project taken from *Paula Pryke's Wreaths & Garlands*, © 1998

page 90 Patchwork duvet cover
Project taken from *Vintage Fabric Style* by Lucinda Ganderton and Rose Hammick, © 2003

page 94 Child's quilt
Project taken from *Vintage Fabric Style* by Lucinda Ganderton and Rose Hammick, © 2003

acknowledgments

With thanks to Miriam for making the writing process
so pleasant and easy. And with love to my wonderful
family – especially Martin, Felix and Tegan.